Penguin Health
Osteopathy for Everyone

Paul Masters studied and received his DO (Diploma of Osteopathy) from the Natural Therapeutic and Osteopathic Society and Register in 1978. He was awarded a fellowship of the Society in 1983 for his unceasing contributions towards osteopathic education and has recently been appointed Vice-Principal and Director of Osteopathic Principles and Techniques to the London School of Osteopathy.

He is also well known in Europe and has lectured extensively in Belgium on the principles of osteopathic manipulation. For this he was in 1985 awarded the Diploma of Osteopathic Medicine and honorary membership of the Association of Belgian Osteopaths.

In between teaching and lecturing he manages to run a busy and successful practice in Westcliff-on-Sea and is regarded by many of his colleagues as one of the most informed practitioners in his field.

PAUL MASTERS

OSTEOPATHY FOR EVERYONE

PENGUIN BOOKS

To my wife and two sons –
for their love and support

PENGUIN BOOKS

Published by the Penguin Group
27 Wrights Lane, London w8 5TZ, England
Viking Penguin Inc., 40 West 23rd Street, New York, New York 10010, USA
Penguin Books Australia Ltd, Ringwood, Victoria, Australia
Penguin Books Canada Ltd, 2801 John Street, Markham, Ontario, Canada L3R 1B4
Penguin Books (NZ) Ltd, 182–190 Wairau Road, Auckland 10, New Zealand

Penguin Books Ltd, Registered Offices: Harmondsworth, Middlesex, England

First published 1988

The figure on p. 81 is after J. Marshall Hoag, *Osteopathic Medicine*
(McGraw-Hill), copyright © J. Marshall Hoag, 1969. Reproduced
by permission

Made and printed in Great Britain by
Richard Clay Ltd, Bungay, Suffolk
Filmset in 11/13 Monophoto Plantin

CONTENTS

ACKNOWLEDGEMENTS

I would like to thank all those who have made this book possible. Especially my wife, who typed the original script and gave support and constructive advice when necessary, my father, Mr A. F. E. Masters, MBE, who patiently read through the script, Anthea Courtenay Ridett for her constructive criticism and editorial experience, Mr Peter Jarvis, DO, MNTOS, for his photographic work, Mr Victor Foster, DO, MBNOA, for his help, advice and teaching during my early years in practice, the Institute for Complementary Medicine, for their support and good work within the Complementary Therapies, and lastly, but certainly not least, all osteopaths who have contributed to osteopathy and whose knowledge I have drawn on to write this book.

CHAPTER ONE

AN INTRODUCTION

TO OSTEOPATHY

Osteopathy is probably best known to the general public as a system of manipulation to treat aches and pains in the spine, muscles and joints – the framework of the body known as the musculoskeletal system. Most osteopaths would regard it as a far wider ranging therapy than this. It was founded in America in the late nineteenth century by a medical reformer, Dr Andrew Taylor Still. Dr Still was of the opinion that the human body has a natural ability to heal itself, that poor health and disease could result from misalignments in the musculoskeletal framework, and the whole body. In this book I hope to familiarize the reader with that correct manipulation could not only restore this system to its proper balance, but also encourage the body's own self-healing mechanisms to restore general health.

In the early days of osteopathy there were some who claimed that it was a panacea, a cure-all; this was something of an exaggeration, and the orthodox medical profession rightly rejected it as such. However, osteopaths today have not lost sight of Dr Still's concept that physiological function – the way in which the body works – depends upon what osteopaths refer to as 'structural integrity': that is, the correct alignment and balance of the musculoskeletal system. This implies far more than simply the treatment of bad backs.

Since its inception osteopathy has become a highly efficient system of diagnosis and treatment of the musculoskeletal system. It is directed towards releasing muscles, soft tissue and joint casualties by applying selected manipulative techniques with the minimum of force. However, while it is mainly directed to the musculoskeletal system, osteopathy can have a far-reaching effect on the whole body. In this book I hope to familiarize the reader with the vast therapeutic range of which osteopathy is capable.

The Scope of Osteopathy

Since the musculoskeletal system represents sixty per cent of the entire body mass, it is not surprising that osteopaths emphasize its importance in both health and disease. This is not to say that all diseases are caused by musculoskeletal problems: disease is usually the result of multiple factors, in which the musculoskeletal system is often involved. But osteopaths feel that at present there is a gap in general medicine, which does not incorporate osteopathic principles into diagnosis and treatment.

To begin with, the mobility of the musculoskeletal system is very important to our health, and it is an area in which I find great variations when examining my patients. One expects differences between the very young and the very old, but a comparison between several people of the same age can be surprising. Some show normal patterns for their age, while others are so stiff and immobile that they could be ten or fifteen years older – hence the saying 'you are as old as your spine'. And the general health of those people with less mobility is usually poorer than those who display a normal degree of suppleness in their movements.

This mobility depends not only on the bones, joints, ligaments and muscles; much of the musculoskeletal system is made up of connective tissues. These take the form of sheets or bands of fibres gathered together; among their main functions they support, bind and protect the muscles, joints and various organs, and provide some stability between the joints. Without them we would literally fall apart!

In osteopathy much importance is given to these connective tissues, or fascia. Still described them as a 'rich hunting ground' in the study of the many diseases of man. In addition to their supportive role, they have other important functions. For example, they also play a role in metabolism, and in the body's

Figure 1. The function of all vital organs is controlled by the spinal nerves. These nerves also act as a pathway along which problems in the various organs or the spine can be relayed to the opposite end of the spinal communication system. Recently studies have indicated that some of these 'reflections' along the spinal nerves may cause permanent damage to the organ at the end of the communication pathway.

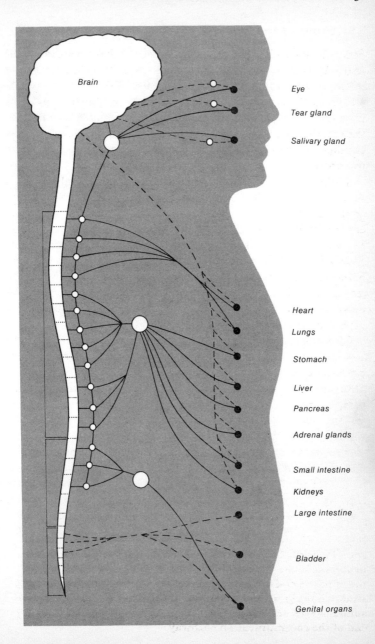

Brain

Eye

Tear gland

Salivary gland

Heart

Lungs

Stomach

Liver

Pancreas

Adrenal glands

Small intestine

Kidneys

Large intestine

Bladder

Genital organs

defensive system. An important characteristic of the fascia is their ability to stretch and contract; this can alter with the advance of time, and their elasticity may decrease, playing a part in the loss of normal mobility that occurs during the ageing process.

The musculoskeletal system can also be likened to a mirror: it actually reflects disorders within our bodies. This is because it is linked to other bodily systems via the circulatory and nervous systems, the two vital channels of communication which connect and unify the whole body. Thus if there is some disorder, say, within the visceral system – the inner organs – this will be reflected through to the musculoskeletal system in the form of tension and pain. This phenomenon was first recognized within the medical profession by Sir James Mackenzie, a cardiologist and physician born in Scotland in 1853, who practised in Burnley and London. He observed that people suffering with heart disease constantly showed areas of tenderness in the upper thoracic spine (the area of the spine just below the neck). Other tender areas in and around the spine have since been identified with visceral malfunctions and pathologies such as gall-bladder and kidney problems.

Osteopaths are firmly convinced that the reverse also happens: that is, injuries to the musculoskeletal system, particularly those that osteopaths refer to as 'spinal lesions' (see Chapter 3), can contribute to a malfunction or cause further problems to an already diseased or stressed internal organ. Excessive emotions such as anxiety, depression, fear, and even too much joy can also cause tensions that reflect through to the musculoskeletal system.

The musculoskeletal system will be described in greater detail with reference to the various painful syndromes and complaints, but from this brief overview the reader will appreciate that by releasing musculoskeletal tensions and, when possible, restoring the system to normal, osteopathic treatment can have beneficial influences on the body as a whole. This means that it is not only an effective treatment for localized disorders and pain, but can enhance and contribute to the maintenance of general health.

There are many people who are not acutely ill, or who are not sick enough to prevent them performing their daily duties and activities, yet who do not feel or behave with the liveliness and energy associated with optimum health. A large number have come to accept this lowered vitality and diminished health, and have learned to live with or ignore their chronic aches and pains. In my opinion, applying osteopathic treatment to the musculoskeletal system could help people like this to realize their full health potential.

The modern-day osteopath can modify his* approach to benefit all kinds of people; in my own practice I treat a wide range of patients, from babyhood to old age, from the very frail to the very robust, suffering from a variety of complaints. Osteopathy can also relieve numerous problems by stimulating the body's inherent defensive mechanisms. As well as the common rheumatic and arthritic complaints and the inevitable low-back and neck problems, these include many conditions for which people might not normally think of consulting an osteopath, such as migraine, sinusitis, certain skin conditions, asthma, and some forms of high blood pressure, to name but a few.

In recent years, too, osteopathy has been playing a useful role in sports injuries, and has become popular with many top sportsmen and women. Only recently I successfully treated a sportsman who had previously been diagnosed as having a hamstring strain. This had been treated over some time by a physiotherapist with a combination of ultrasound, interferential therapy† and exercises; however, his condition only finally responded when osteopathic treatment was given to the pelvis and lumbar spine.

Of course, osteopathy cannot cure every illness, and osteopaths must recognize their limitations. There are some diseases which it is not appropriate to treat, not because treatment would necessarily be harmful, but because they simply do not respond to osteopathy.

There are also some conditions for which osteopathy is definitely contra-indicated. For example, it would be foolish and wrong for an osteopath to apply forceful manipulation to any

* As I have written this book from my own viewpoint, the masculine form has been adopted, though acknowledgement is of course due to the large body of women osteopaths.

†A method of discharging low-frequency impulses into the body to relieve pain, increase blood flow and lymphatic circulation and stimulate the motor nerves.

area where the tissue is weakened by active bone disease, where there is evidence of pressure on the spinal cord, or where there is a risk of possible circulatory injury through, for example, very advanced arteriosclerosis (hardening of the arteries). Recognizing and diagnosing such conditions form part of the osteopath's training, which makes osteopathy a very safe form of treatment. The osteopath is also trained in a wide range of manipulative methods, so that in those conditions for which it would be unwise to use forceful types of manipulation, he can still help by performing other, more gentle, manipulative contacts.

It is only through good training and much study that the osteopaths are able to apply their art correctly and deal with a wide scope of ailments. And they do get good results, so that recovered patients recommend their services to others seeking help. Consequently, osteopathy is becoming more and more popular with the British public.

Osteopathy Compared with other Forms of Manipulation

There are a number of other forms of treatment which incorporate manual manipulations into their regime. Let us take a brief look at some of these.

Chiropractic. I am frequently asked by patients and friends about the difference between osteopathy and chiropractic. In fact, the two systems are similar in many respects. Both treat the spine by manipulation, and they share the fundamental philosophy that manipulation not only relieves pain but also can improve the patient's general health.

The word chiropractic is derived from two Greek words, *cheiro praktikos*, meaning 'done by hand'. It is a system of treating human ailments by manual adjustments, primarily to the spine, although other parts of the body may be included such as the feet, knees, ribs and elbows. Chiropractic was founded in 1895, some twenty years after osteopathy, by a man called Daniel David Palmer in Iowa, USA.

The story of the very first chiropractic treatment is well known. Palmer was talking with a caretaker called Harvey Willard, who had been deaf ever since injuring his spine some seventeen years before. Palmer examined the man's spine and found a very painful area where a vertebra was misaligned. Palmer explained to him that he believed that the spinal problem was associated with the deafness, and asked his permission to re-align the bone. This he did by thrusting with the heel of his hand directly against the vertebra, restoring its normal alignment and also, almost

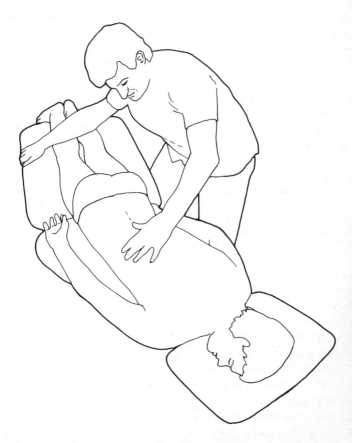

Figure 2. The osteopathic couch in use. A lever is released allowing the lower leaf of the table to side-bend while the osteopath offers counterforce to the spine. This is performed in a rhythmical manner to improve circulation and liberate the spinal areas.

miraculously it seemed, restoring the caretaker's hearing. This adjustment was based on Palmer's theory that the misalignment of a vertebra – which Palmer called a 'subluxation' – could interfere with the correct function of the nervous system.

At one time osteopaths and chiropractors regarded each other as enemies; in the early days, each group claimed that the other stole and copied their techniques. This negative attitude has changed through the years to one of friendly rivalry, and now osteopaths and chiropractors work together much more closely.

One of the main differences remaining between the two lies in the application of technique. Firstly, the osteopath generally spends more time using a massage-type technique called soft-tissue manipulation; this is nearly always given prior to specific joint manipulation. Chiropractors tend to do less soft-tissue work, often preferring to go straight into the spinal adjustment. Osteopaths feel that soft-tissue manipulation is an essential part of the treatment; when performed correctly and specifically it helps prepare the tissues by releasing the muscular tensions surrounding the involved joint; only a minimal amount of force is then needed to apply a manipulative thrust.

There is also a difference between the type of thrusts used. The chiropractor uses his hands in more direct contact on the joints of the vertebrae than does the osteopath. For example, in dealing with a spinal problem in the lower back the osteopath, using traditional methods, will adjust with the patient lying on their side; he will then rotate the patient's upper torso one way while rotating the pelvis in the opposite direction, at the same time feeling for reduced movement at the specific vertebrae involved. When the body has been manoeuvred so that the spine is locked above and below the specific area, a light high-speed thrust is made with the forearm which is resting across the pelvic bone. The intention of this manipulative manoeuvre is to liberate the restriction within the spinal joint.

The chiropractor, on the other hand, will have the patient lying face down with the head resting in the mid-line (normally a hole is built into the couch in which the patient can rest his head). The chiropractor then makes contact with specific points

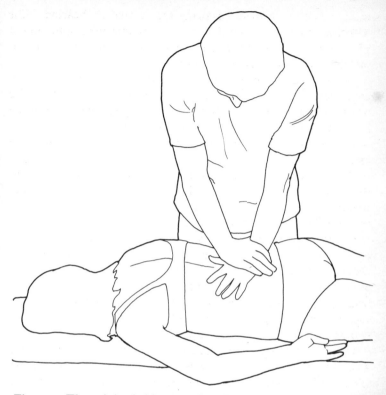

Figure 3. The original chiropractic adjustment developed by the founder, Daniel Palmer. The adjusting hand directs the force against the spinous process: the thrust is made in a downward and slightly lateral direction.

of his hands directly on to the subluxated vertebra, and performs a thrust to re-align it.

Another of the main differences between the two professions is the use of X-rays. Chiropractors believe that X-ray examination is an essential part of examination and diagnosis; the majority have their own X-ray facilities and will X-ray most patients on the first visit, or arrange for the patients to see a radiographer. Osteopaths, on the other hand, do not use X-rays as a matter of routine, although they do use them when they consider it necessary, or as a confirmation of their clinical diagnosis. If there is any doubt or uncertainty regarding pathological or contra-indicative conditions to manipulative osteopathic treatment, then the osteopath will not hesitate to obtain an X-ray examination before giving any treatment.

However, although there are some basic differences like these, it is fair to say that some techniques overlap between both professions. A person who visits both for treatment may not necessarily notice the subtle differences in the application of technique.

As to the question of who gets the best and quickest results, since I am an osteopath I am liable to say the osteopath, and I should expect chiropractors to say that they get best results! However, to be factual and fair-minded, the effectiveness of the two systems is probably about equal. Results may well depend on the individual patient's preference and the individual skills of the practitioner.

Massage. Rubbing an injured part of the body is an instinctive human action. Massage has nearly always been included in the ancient forms of medicine, including both western and oriental systems. One of the earliest documentations of massage is found in Chinese literature of about 2700 BC. The Greek physician Hippocrates (460–360 BC) advocated the use of frictional massage movements for certain conditions. It was through the influence of the Greeks that massage became popular and was practised in Rome. Julius Caesar, in the first century BC, apparently had himself 'pinched all over' daily to rid him of neuralgia.

One of the first people to transform massage into a therapeutic system was Pehr Henrik Ling (1776–1839) who founded the Swedish System of Gymnastics and Massage. But it was not until late into the nineteenth century that the benefits of massage began to be recognized by the medical profession, mostly through the work of a Dr Mezger of Amsterdam. He instructed and taught doctors in the art and principles of massage; his clinical results in treating conditions by this technique were so good that he gained respect from many doctors all over the world.

Massage is widely used today for its many therapeutic benefits, and it can be an effective form of inducing relaxation and reducing stress in the musculoskeletal framework. Undoubtedly, one of its main benefits is to improve the circulation, relieving the congestion and oedema that can occur as a result of injuries to muscles and soft tissues.

Massage is entirely different from osteopathy. Osteopathy is a system of medicine, not a technique.

Bone-setting. The ancient form of manipulation used to be particularly popular and prominent in England. 'Bone-setters' were people who practised crude forms of manipulation to re-align bones supposedly out of position. Their methods were usually handed down from father to son; they were kept as closely guarded family secrets, and the techniques were not usually written down or spoken about.

Many bone-setters certainly had a genuine natural ability, and they often obtained excellent results in allaying people's aches and pains. One of the most famous in the past was a Mrs Mapp who lived in the eighteenth century; she was asked to treat a spinal deformity in the niece of Sir Hans Sloane, a member of the College of Physicians and the first doctor to be honoured with a knighthood.

There are still a few bone-setters practising today, mainly in country districts. Bone-setting is a far cry from osteopathic manipulation, which is based on certain principles and specific diagnosis; in comparison the bone-setter's manipulations are crude and clumsy.

Physiotherapy. The physiotherapist generally treats the patient by physical means, employing such techniques as the application of heat, cold, electrotherapy, exercise, massage, traction and manipulation.

To the onlooker, some of the manipulations employed may look similar to osteopathic techniques; this is not surprising as the manipulative physiotherapists have adopted techniques from both chiropractic and osteopathy. However, this is where the similarity ends. The manipulation practised by physiotherapists is employed with a different philosophy in mind to that of osteopathy, in as much as it is applied only to the specific locality of pain and trouble. The osteopath has a totally different outlook; he applies his manipulative techniques from a holistic mechanistic viewpoint: that is, looking at the musculoskeletal system as a whole, which often involves treating other areas than the obvious site of pain.

Medical Manipulation. There are two main avenues open to the doctor wishing to learn manipulation at post-graduate level. One is the London College of Osteopathic Medicine, which offers a thirteen-week course in osteopathic principles and manipulation taken over one year. There is also a course offered by the British Association of Manipulative Medicine (BAMM), consisting of nine weekends learning manipulation techniques alone; BAMM has about three hundred members.

The highest number of medically qualified practitioners practising manipulative therapy in Europe is in Germany, where there are some 2,500.

Manipulation Under Anaesthetic. This is performed by orthopaedic surgeons, usually within the hospital operating theatre. A light general anaesthesia is given so that the patient is not conscious and has no control over his or her muscular system. This type of manipulation is usually only employed after other conventional methods have failed. When applied to the lower back this is normally because the surgeon believes that 'adhesions' (fibrous tissues) have formed around the joint. If he suspects disc herniation or rupture – the so-called 'slipped disc' (see Chapter 7) – he will generally consider surgery.

This approach to manipulation does have its drawbacks. Firstly, it cannot be repeated frequently and so success has to rely heavily on the one manipulation. Secondly, there is the problem that the body of an unconscious patient is like a rag doll, offering no muscle resistance. This does away with any natural muscle guarding to protect against over-forceful movements, and since too much force could further damage the tissues, the manipulation has to be performed extremely carefully. Generally, I would not recommend this method of manipulation – though having said this, I had one case of a frozen shoulder that had reached a plateau under my care, which was further improved by manipulation under anaesthetic.

CHAPTER TWO

OSTEOPATHY

PAST AND PRESENT

It could be said that Andrew Taylor Still first discovered osteopathy when he was only ten years old. As a boy he frequently suffered from very bad headaches, from which he could find no relief. Then one day he laid the back of his head and neck across a blanketed plough line, a rope suspended between two trees, about eight to ten inches above the ground. After a short time lying on his back in this position he became quite comfortable and soon fell asleep. When he woke he found to his delight that his headache had completely gone. From that day on he would repeat this procedure whenever a headache troubled him, and on each occasion experienced total relief.

Many years later, after he had acquired some knowledge of anatomy and physiology, Dr Still realized that the relief provided by this form of self-treatment came about by inhibiting the action of the great occipital nerves (which are situated at the back of the skull) and improving the flow of arterial blood to and through the veins. It contributed to his formulation of the theory that 'the rule of the artery is supreme', meaning that good health depended on the circulation of the blood, while any interference with blood flow could lead to impaired health or disease. (It should be said here that modern osteopaths realize that there can be multiple causes of disease, and that interference in the normal blood flow is only one of these possible causes.)

Born in Virginia in 1828, Andrew Taylor Still became interested in medicine and healing under the influence of his father, Abraham Still, who was both a preacher and a doctor. Much of Still's early medical education was gained by serving an apprenticeship under his father. He also went through the customary form of medical training for that time, which was 'reading' medicine. This enabled him to qualify and become a licensed Medical

Doctor in the state of Missouri. He also studied for a short time at the College of Physicians and Surgeons in Kansas City, Missouri.

The practice of medicine at the time was often crude, including remedies such as bleeding, purging and blistering, and drugs were used in a heavy-handed fashion. During the Civil War, Still served as a surgeon in the Union Army, and became extremely distressed at the number of deaths that occurred through inadequate medical treatment. He was horrified at the large numbers of surgical operations and amputations which were performed under terrible conditions – there were as yet no anaesthetics and no knowledge of antiseptics or bacterial infection. Still began to wonder if there might not be an alternative method of treating human ills, diseases and pain.

These thoughts remained with him after the war had ended. Then, in 1864, he found himself watching helplessly as three of his children died during an epidemic of spinal meningitis. This personal tragedy finally turned him away from orthodox medicine, totally disillusioned with the medical drugs, remedies and theories of the time.

Dr Still spent the next ten years of his life searching for a new, better form of medicine. He started by looking at nature itself, seeking the cause of ill-health within the human body. He first studied the human bone structure, digging up Indian graves to provide the research material he needed. From his autobiography it is clear that it disturbed him to have to do this, but he felt that his actions were justified by the good that came from them, in the form of a new concept of natural medicine which was to bring relief to many sufferers.

He began to develop the theory that the body has natural powers of self-healing, and he became particularly interested in the circulation of the blood, which he called 'the river of life'. From there, he came to the conclusion that misalignments in the musculoskeletal framework, particularly the spine, could impede the blood flow, impairing the self-healing mechanism and acting as a prime cause of poor health and disease. He found that by applying manipulative pressures with his hands he could stimulate self-healing. To bring about good health it was therefore imperative to improve, restore and maintain the correct alignment of the musculoskeletal framework. This concept he termed 'maintaining structural integrity'.

Researching these theories and putting them into practice, Still developed what he came to call osteopathy, derived from the Greek words 'osteo', meaning bone (since bones were the first structures of the body that he studied), and 'pathos', meaning suffering. An integral part of his new system of medicine was always to seek the cause of his patients' problems, as opposed to just treating symptoms with drugs. He was also convinced that any form of medicine must be practised under strictly hygienic conditions.

Dr Still's theories had much in common with those of the Greek physician and philosopher Hippocrates, who had taught in the fourth century BC that physicians should treat the person, rather than the disease. Still shared Hippocrates' belief that each patient should be treated as an individual, and that not just the symptoms of disease should be considered, but also the nature of the person. In Ancient Greece, many of Hippocrates' theories gave way to the Cnidian theories of medicine, which emphasized specific treatments for specific diseases, leading to a medical system in which disease and its symptoms were regarded as more important than the patient.

In the late nineteenth century, the science of medicine was being added to and updated, mostly in Europe, by new discoveries and new theories. These included Pasteur's theory of germs, Virchow's cellular pathology, Ehrlich's theory of immunity, Koch's advances in bacteriology, Lister's discovery of antiseptic surgery, and Bernard's contributions to physiology. All these theories were being developed at about the time that Still was developing his ideas in America. At the same time, Sir William Osler was influencing medical education in England. He had similar ideas to those of Still, placing the chief emphasis on treating the individual and, like Still, opposing the unnecessary prescribing of drugs.

Nevertheless, Still's theories brought him much criticism from many members of the orthodox medical profession, who derided his idea that manipulation of the spine could affect the general health. He was labelled a quack and a charlatan; even so-called friends turned their backs on him. Undeterred, he became relentless in spreading his theories and concepts and practising his new system. He would travel the country, curing and helping the sick; many people were eager for him to use his skills on them. His reputation grew as a man who could bring about miraculous cures by using his hands, and people would travel many miles to obtain his services.

In Still's two books, *Philosophy of Osteopathy* and his autobiography, he listed many conditions that could be cured by osteopathy. They included asthma, appendicitis, fevers, headaches, and fits, as well as the usual neck, lower back and extremity pains. For example, in *Philosophy of Osteopathy* he writes:

Can consumption be cured? If you have a tiresome and weakening cough at the close of winter, and wish to be cured, we would advise you to begin osteopathic treatment at once, so that the lungs can heal and harden against next winter's attack. This is the first I have written on 'consumption' because I wanted to test my conclusions by long and careful observations on cases that I have taken and successfully treated. I kept the results from the public print until I could obtain positive proof that consumption could be cured. So far the discovered causes give me little doubt, and the cures are a certainty in very many cases. An early beginning is one of the great considerations in incipient consumption. (Still, 1977, pp. 73–4.)

Soon, Still had more patients than he could manage, and it became obvious to him that there was a need for an osteopathic school, where others could learn his system of medicine. With this in mind, he first approached Baker University, a medical institution in his home town of Balwin, Kansas, which he and his two brothers had helped to build and found. Despite this connection, he was refused admission, on the grounds that his theories did not conform to the University's own medical theories.

Very disappointed but undeterred, he left Kansas and went to Missouri. There, although opposed by many medical doctors, he continued to treat people with osteopathy. Many of his patients experienced such quick relief from their various ailments that he was nicknamed 'the lightning bone-setter'. At last, in 1892, in Kirksville, Missouri, he opened the American School of Osteopathy, which by 1902 had around five hundred students. It still exists today, now known as the Kirksville College of Osteopathic Medicine. In 1892 it was granted a charter under the governing law of Missouri, which recognized it as a scientific institution. In 1894 another charter was obtained, this time establishing it as an osteopathic medical college.

This second charter was very important in the history of American osteopathy, since it allowed the American School of Osteopathy to award a medical degree as conferred by other reputable medical colleges. However, Dr Still decided against awarding an MD degree to graduates from the American School of Osteopathy, preferring to use the new designation of DO, Diplomate of Osteopathy. Although the school's medical curriculum was comparable with that of other medical schools at the time, he regarded the distinction as important, since his graduates differed from normal MDs in their use of manipulation and osteopathic principles as their main treatment approach to patients.

From this first school, other colleges of osteopathy opened up. Some were dubious in nature, operating mainly for profit rather than for the good of osteopathy. Some were run by correspondence, with no contact teaching whatsoever; others issued diplomas which were not worth the paper they were written on! This led to great concern within the profession, and in 1898 the bona fide schools met in Kirksville to set up standards and to regulate their profession. They formed an association called the Associated Colleges of Osteopathy, which managed to bring about the closure of some of the dubious schools, while osteopathic courses were extended from two to three years.

The next turning-point in the American history of osteopathy was the so-called independent Flexner Report. Abraham Flexner was responsible for investigating both the allopathic (orthodox) and the non-orthodox medical schools. In the last he included both osteopathic and homoeopathic schools; he did not see fit even to consider including either the chiropractors or mechanotherapists (another form of manipulative therapy) as part of a medical system.

Flexner found many problems existing within the osteopathic colleges. He criticized them for accepting students who did not hold High School diplomas, and found that the technical teaching was lacking in dissection studies, laboratory facilities and clinical practice. It was not just the osteopathic colleges that came in for criticism; many of the medical colleges also were deficient, and Flexner recommended that out of 155 of these colleges, only thirty-one should be allowed to continue.

The Flexner Report, published in 1910, brought about some positive changes in medical practice. Both the allopathic and the osteopathic schools and colleges upgraded their standards, bringing them into line with the Report's recommendations.

Osteopathic legislation took place from state to state, granting osteopaths equal status with medical doctors. One of the first bills was put forward in 1895, but it was opposed and blocked, mainly by the orthodox medical profession. Another, put forward in 1897 for Washington DC, was successful and became law. Gradually legislation was achieved in each of the states, despite strong opposition from the medical profession. The following story highlights the sort of opposition osteopathy had to contend with. It took place at a hearing before the Joint Committee on New York Legislation on 28 February 1901. A surgeon was representing and arguing the case for medical physicians in opposition to the osteopaths. He brought forward the cadaver of a small child and challenged the osteopathic representative to manipulate the spinal vertebrae in lesion – his purpose being to prove that spinal lesions did not exist. The osteopath refused to oblige; instead, he challenged the surgeon to give the cadaver a laxative to see if he could make its bowels move!

Following the formation of the Association of Osteopathic Colleges, a new organization came into being. This was the American Osteopathic Association, whose chief purpose was to promote osteopathy for the good of public health, and to maintain and upgrade, when needed, the medical education within osteopathic colleges.

When World War I broke out, another battle took place between the DOs and the MDs. The osteopaths offered their skills to their country during this troubled time, and the doctors opposed this, regarding them as inferior physicians. Despite strong public backing for the osteopaths, the doctors won the day by threatening to withdraw their services from the armed forces to whom the osteopaths were offering help.

At the start of World War II the American Medical Association once again blocked the efforts of the DOs to become involved within the Medical Corps. This time, however, the osteopaths used the situation to their advantage by giving excellent care to the civilian population, which gained them acceptance and made them many new friends and supporters.

Post-war, in California, the American Medical Association made another move which might have enabled them to take over the osteopathic movement in the USA. This consisted of giving accreditation to the existing College of Osteopathic Physicians and Surgeons, but renaming it 'The California College of Medicine'. The majority of DOs in California agreed to this move, and were given MD degrees for sixty-five dollars. However, a small minority decided to remain loyal to their profession and refused.

In 1962 a new bill was passed for the state of California, refusing admission to any new DO osteopaths. This caused the osteopaths a great deal of concern; they feared that similar action might be adopted by other states. However, the American Osteopathic Association made advantageous use of this action by acquiring legislation within those states that had not previously accepted the lawful full freedom of practice for osteopaths. They argued that if the majority (2,400 osteopaths) were eligible for a doctor's degree in medicine, this must surely mean that the qualifications of DO and MD were of equal status. They also made the point that if DOs were competent to practise general medicine in California they must also be competent to practise elsewhere. This argument won the day, and in 1974 a licence for osteopaths to practise was re-established in California.

Today, osteopathy in America has become accepted within the medical profession and osteopaths everywhere have equal status with medical doctors. The American osteopath takes the same exams as the orthodox doctor, apart from the addition of manipulative therapy. There are fourteen osteopathic colleges, whose graduates, after a four-year training, are licensed to practise by all the American states. Unfortunately, more and more American osteopaths are using less and less manipulative therapy in the care of their patients, and a high proportion of them prescribe drugs. One of the main reasons for this is that the American MD is a vanishing species; many of them have left general practice to specialize in other branches of medicine. In taking over the role of traditional family doctor (as chiropractors have also done), American osteopaths have acquired a greater workload. Faced with a large number of patients, it takes much less time and effort to write a prescription than to examine and treat the musculoskeletal system.

In 1974 Professor Irvin Korr, PhD, a researcher who has probably contributed more to osteopathy than anyone since Andrew Taylor Still, sounded a warning note in an address to the American osteopathic profession. He pointed out that in the course of its long struggle for recognition the profession appeared to have forgotten why it sought recognition in the first place – to enable it to deliver and demonstrate as widely and fully as possible the benefits of osteopathic principles and methods. In forgetting its purpose, the profession had permitted osteopathic manipulation to slip from its place as a key element in osteopathic practice.

Osteopathy in the United Kingdom

Osteopathy was introduced to the UK in the early 1900s by a disciple of Andrew Taylor Still, a Scot named John Martin Littlejohn, who studied under Still at the American School of Osteopathy. Before leaving America he founded the Chicago College of Osteopathic Medicine, which is still in existence today. In 1917 he founded the first school of osteopathy in the UK, the British School of Osteopathy, now the largest training establishment in the UK. Littlejohn taught osteopathy from a holistic point of view: to get the patient better the osteopath must look at and adjust imbalances not only on a mechanical level, but also on nutritional, psychological and environmental levels. These principles are just as important in osteopathic practice today.

As in America, osteopathy in the UK has had its share of
opposition from the medical profession, particularly in the early
days when osteopaths were inclined to make claims for cures that
appeared to be medically impossible. Over the years, however,
osteopathy has proved itself as a safe and effective treatment for
musculoskeletal problems, and today a number of medical doctors
both refer patients to osteopaths and receive osteopathic
treatment themselves. There are now several osteopathic training
colleges in the UK, some offering full-time four-year courses,
others offering a part-time training over a longer period in order
to cover a similar syllabus. (Details of these schools are given in
the Appendix.)

There is naturally some rivalry between the different schools;
on the whole this can only be for the good both of osteopathy and
the general public, since a sense of competition encourages them
to establish and maintain the highest possible standards of education. The important question, however, is not which has the
slight edge over the other, but that a high standard of osteopathic
training is conducted at every school, ensuring that their graduates are competent to practise independently of, but complementary to, orthodox medicine.

There is one area, however, where the rivalry between the
schools has acted to the disadvantage of the profession, and that
is the question of legal status. In the UK osteopathy is in an
unusual, somewhat strange situation. For while it appears to be
accepted by the majority of the public – and I do not think there
is any dispute that a large number of people have been and are
being helped by osteopathic treatment – its practitioners have so
far been unable to obtain lawful recognition and acceptance.

Like other alternative practitioners in the UK, osteopaths
practise under Common Law. Although the different schools
publish registers of their qualified members, there is no *statutory*
register for all osteopaths in the UK. Common Law allows
freedom of practice, and freedom for members of the public to
choose by whom they will be treated; at the same time, it does
not protect them from charlatans. In fact, anybody can call themselves an osteopath with no training whatsoever, or set up and
practise after taking a few weekends' instruction. Dr John

Ebbetts, President of the Natural Therapeutic and Osteopathic Society, tells how he treated a man who was employed as a coalman: shortly afterwards the man opened up in the same town as an osteopath!

The osteopathic profession has no protection against the charlatans who abuse it by incorrectly practising what they call 'osteopathy' in ignorance of its true principles, which can on occasions lead to poor results, if not worse. Osteopathy does not consist of treating two, three or four people all at the same time, by wiring them up to therapy machines or placing them under hot lamps. Nor does it comprise giving any form of manipulation without conducting a prior consultation and thorough examination to arrive at a diagnosis. People who treat the public in this way give osteopathy a bad name.

Fortunately, such people are in the minority, and generally speaking osteopaths are well-trained, over a four-year full-time or five- to six-year part-time course. Most are sincere and responsible people dedicated to relieving pain and restoring health, and offering genuine help whenever they can.

Legislation to give osteopaths legal status in the UK would have several advantages. It would necessitate standardizing training and qualifications, and introducing an overall Code of Ethics; this would help to protect the public from charlatans and make it easier for doctors to refer patients to osteopaths with confidence. It would also, hopefully, enable osteopathic students to obtain grants more easily. Although some local authorities do make discretionary grants, all the schools and colleges are self-supporting and most students have to pay their own way – which is the main reason for the existence of the part-time schools. Other benefits might follow, such as the right for osteopaths to refer patients direct for blood-tests and X-rays, which would save patients time, money and inconvenience.

The first moves to have osteopathy recognized within the law were made as early as 1923, when Mr W. A. Streeter, an osteopath, founded the Osteopathic Defence League for this purpose. The first Osteopaths' Bill was agreed and introduced into the House of Lords in 1931. It failed to become law, basically because the two osteopathic bodies of the day, the Defence League and the British Osteopathic Association, were in disagreement between themselves.

The next attempt was in 1935, when a bill to regulate and register osteopaths was put before a select committee of the House of Lords. This time the osteopaths themselves were more unified: the bodies involved were the British Osteopathic Association, Mr Streeter's Osteopathic Defence League, the Incorporated Association of Osteopaths and the British School of Osteopathy. The inquiry lasted twelve days, but the outcome was not favourable to the osteopaths, the biggest stumbling-blocks being the definition of osteopathy and the category of diseases which it could treat; this bill also failed.

On 7 April 1976 Mrs Joyce Butler, MP, presented a Bill (No. 113) in the House of Commons in an attempt once again to secure official recognition for osteopaths. Unfortunately, the bill only listed three osteopathic training establishments, the British School of Osteopathy, the British College of Naturopathy and Osteopathy and the London College of Osteopathy, which gives a one-year training to doctors. Excluded from the bill were some other osteopathic establishments which had good standards of training and, like the three organizations involved, also held private registers of qualified, competent osteopathic practitioners; one of these was the Natural Therapeutic and Osteopathic Society and Register. This exclusion aroused suspicions within the profession, and the lack of unity within the osteopathic movement as a whole resulted in enormous opposition to the bill in the House of Commons; it did not receive a second reading.

Another Osteopaths' Bill (No. 218) was presented recently, on 23 July 1986. Its aim was to establish the existing General Council and Register of Osteopaths (GCRO) as the statutory registering and governing body: 'to unite and regulate the practice of osteopathy and certain other practitioners of manipulative therapy; to restrict the practice thereof by unqualified persons other than registered Medical Practitioners and state-registered physiotherapists and for connected purposes'.

This Bill, like the others, did not get as far as a second reading. I believe that it was premature; although it was presented in favour of the GCRO, the largest single register in the UK, other bona fide osteopathic professional associations and registers were not informed of its presentation beforehand, which once again has caused some distrust within the profession. However, the Bill has served a useful purpose by instigating fruitful meetings within the profession and by making positive progress towards unification. Meanwhile, the osteopathic profession has been told by the government to 'get its act together' before official recognition can be contemplated, and this, I feel, is now beginning to happen. The Natural Therapeutic and Osteopathic Society and Register, for whom I can speak personally since I am a Council Member, welcomes any sincere steps towards unity within our profession.

More positive headway towards unification is being made in Europe, despite the fact that the situation there is even more complex: as well as a variety of schools and associations, the European countries each have their own laws relating to osteopaths and other alternative practitioners, with the result that in some countries osteopaths are practising illegally!

In June 1986 the first European Convention of Osteopathy took place in Brussels. Around forty European associations and colleges were represented; from Britain the organizations represented were the General Council and Register of Osteopaths, the Natural Therapeutic and Osteopathic Society and Register and the British Naturopathic and Osteopathic Association, together with four schools and colleges – the European School of Osteopathy, the British School of Osteopathy, the London School of Osteopathy and the British College of Naturopathy and Osteopathy.

At this first convention, several motions concerning training and its evolution were voted on unanimously. Discussions were held concerning two very important professional bodies, the European Liaison Committee of Osteopaths (CLEO) and the International Academy of Osteopathic Medicine (IAOM). The CLEO's essential aim is to promote a better usage of osteopathic medicine within the community, and to inform the EEC of all that concerns the profession. The IAOM was created in 1984 at the First International Congress of Osteopathic Medicine in Brussels, when a Council of Administration was elected, and there was a re-grouping of osteopaths from all over the world. The IAOM's main aim is to coordinate scientific research into osteopathy and to establish indisputable standards of osteopathy throughout the world.

In November 1986 a second European Convention was held, at which the statutes of the CLEO were worked on and adopted, and national delegations appointed for each European country and for the Central Committee. It is to be hoped that the CLEO will now become an efficient reality. At the same time the various associations present began to discuss the statutes of the IAOM. A valid definition of osteopathic medicine was also worked out and approved by the whole osteopathic representation present. This is reproduced below.

Osteopathic Medicine is a science, an art and a philosophy derived of health care supported by expanding scientific knowledge. Its philosophy embraces the concept of the unity of the living organism's structure and function. Its specificity consists in using a therapeutic mode aiming at reharmonizing the motility and fluctuation relations of the anatomic structures.

Its art is the application of its concepts to the medical practice in all its branches and specialities. Its science includes among others the behavioural, chemical, physical and biological knowledge related to the establishment and maintenance of health as well as the prevention and alleviation of disease.

Osteopathic concepts emphasize the following principles:

1. The human body through a complex equilibrial system tends to be self-regulatory and self-healing in the face of disease processes.
2. The human body is an entity in which structure and function are mutually and reciprocally interdependent.
3. A rational treatment regimen is based on this philosophy and these principles. It favours the structural functional concept in its diagnostic and therapeutic approach by manual therapy.

To the general public all these conventions, committees and discussions may seem a far cry from the purpose for which osteopathy was originally founded. However, I feel that it is very important that the profession within the UK 'gets its act together' and puts its own house in order. I sincerely believe that a positive form of unification will eventually take place, helping us to gain some form of statutory recognition. Although it might appear that this is all we are concerned with, and although osteopaths may hold differing political views, my own experience tells me that we all share a common bond in our concern for our patients and for providing them with the best possible care.

CHAPTER THREE

THE PRINCIPLES

OF OSTEOPATHY

The Osteopathic Concept

Like other forms of complementary medicine, such as acupuncture, chiropractic and homoeopathy, the practice of osteopathy is based on certain holistic principles, which the practitioner incorporates into his system of treatment. In osteopathy, these principles – often referred to as the 'osteopathic concept' – are as follows:

1. The recognition that the body contains its own natural healing powers and self-regulatory mechanisms.
2. That the body is an integrated unit and that all its systems are interrelated.
3. The recognition and importance of the mechanical component in both health and disease.

Let us look at these in more detail. Firstly, as we have already seen, osteopathy recognizes that the human body contains defensive mechanisms by which it can heal and repair itself and which enable it to resist, compensate for, or adapt to, the strains and stresses it encounters during daily life. It can only do this, however, when it is in harmony with the environment, when it has adequate nutrition, and when its structural integrity is sound.

'Structural integrity' is a term used frequently by osteopaths: it refers to the harmonious balance of the musculoskeletal system, the spine, bones, muscles, joints and connective tissue, which compose the structure of the body. The osteopathic theory is that if structural integrity is impaired by any misalignment or imbalance, the body's natural defences will also be impaired. The person will have less resistance to stress, nutritional deficiency or infection, and ill-health may result.

Without the body's ability to heal itself, if we cut a leg or fracture a bone, we would remain permanently injured! Treatment, no matter what kind, would be a waste of time. (It is this that makes the Acquired Immune Deficiency Syndrome, AIDS, such a threat: the reason a cure is so difficult to obtain is that it attacks the immune system, the body's chief defence mechanism.) In his diagnosis and treatment, the osteopath recognizes that a balance must exist within and without the body, and he looks for the reasons why the patient is suffering, why his or her natural defence mechanisms have broken down. Treatment is aimed at restoring the balance, in order to help the body heal itself.

The concept of body unity means that all the parts of the body interrelate and affect one another, so that abnormal structure or function in one area can disturb the structure and function of another. A disturbance within a joint (termed an osteopathic lesion) not only causes pain, tenderness, muscular spasm and tissue inflammation at the site of the lesion, but also can create problems in other areas, via the body's communication systems, the nervous and circulatory circuits.

Take, for example, the pelvis, the base upon which the spinal column rests: any structural misalignment which causes the pelvis to tilt may cause an imbalance in the musculature of the spinal, pelvic and thigh muscles. This may lead to an alteration in leg-lengths. This in turn will not only cause a change in the balance of the spinal column, which will form curvatures to compensate for the tilted base; it will also affect how the person walks and runs, producing stress in the weight-bearing joints, the feet, ankles, hips and knees. Thus, someone consulting an osteopath for low-back pain may be surprised when the practitioner not only examines the area where the pain is, but looks at his whole body, from his head to his feet.

Taking the concept of body unity even further, the musculoskeletal system cannot be separated from the other systems of the body. It is connected to the inner organs, or viscera, via the body's communication systems. So the patient suffering with low-back pain may also experience irregular bowel habits or a change in his urinary output. He may not connect these with his back pain, but such occurrences will not surprise the osteopath, who is fully aware that if one system is disturbed, other systems can become disturbed, too.

An important role in unifying the body's systems is played by the connective tissues, or fascia. Apart from their supportive and binding functions, they play an essential part in the metabolism, the process by which the physical and chemical elements of the body are changed to help regulate functions such as the heart-beat, respiration and temperature. They are in fact regarded as a total organ system: they are also connected with the defensive mechanism, and have the ability to neutralize potentially poison-ous substances in the body by means of specialized cells contained within the connective tissue system.

These tissues are usually highly vascular, which means that they are rich in blood supply. However, abnormal tensions of the fascia can be caused by tense and strained muscles, altered structural alignment, changes in the position of the internal organs, prolonged unnatural postural positions, and changes arising from chemical imbalances. These in turn can interrupt and slow down the normal circulation of blood and lymph (which acts as a kind of cleansing agent in the body, see Chapter 5). When any abnormal tension is placed on the fascia the tissues become thickened, shortened or calcified. (It is important to point out that these changes precede the degenerative changes of arthritis found in the cartilages and bones, and I believe that if they can be rectified in time the onset of arthritis may be pre-vented.)

Osteopathic medicine favours the structural–functional con-cept in diagnosis and treatment. Osteopaths believe that structure and function are reciprocally related. It follows, then, that a mechanical disturbance in the spinal joints can disrupt the normal physiological workings of the body. The mechanical component may either be the sole cause of the problem, or a contributory factor.

This concept was realized by Andrew Taylor Still, when he began to practise osteopathy. He found that not only did alterations in the anatomical structures of the body disturb the normal function of muscles, ligaments, tendons and joints, but also caused functional disturbances of the related circulatory and nervous systems, leading in turn to disorders within the internal organs.

Within the osteopathic profession there is a belief that this structural–functional mechanical concept is still not given enough attention and recognition by the medical profession. By applying the concept correctly, osteopaths are filling an essential gap in the treatment of human disorders. The osteopathic approach is a holistic one: any form of good medicine must consider all the systems of the body in disease, including the musculoskeletal system.

The Spinal Column

Before going any further, it will be helpful to take a brief look at the anatomy of the spine (see Figure 4).

The spinal column is made up of four natural curvatures, consisting as a rule of seven cervical vertebrae (in the neck), twelve thoracic vertebrae (in the upper back), five lumbar vertebrae (in the lower back), and the sacrum, the triangular bone on which the spine sits.* In between the vertebrae, and attached to them, lie the intervertebral discs, which act as shock absorbers and allow the spine to bend and twist.

The spinal column acts as a protective casing for the spinal cord, which is an extension from the brain and which forms a vast relay system for every nerve signal in the body. Within the spinal column, between the vertebrae, are twenty-three pairs of openings called the intervertebral foramina. Through these, nerves, blood vessels and lymphatic vessels pass to and from the spinal cord to every part of the body.

From the occiput, the base of the skull, to the sacro-iliac area

* This is the general rule, but variations can exist. For example, owing to a congenital defect a person could have an extra lumbar vertebra, making six instead of five.

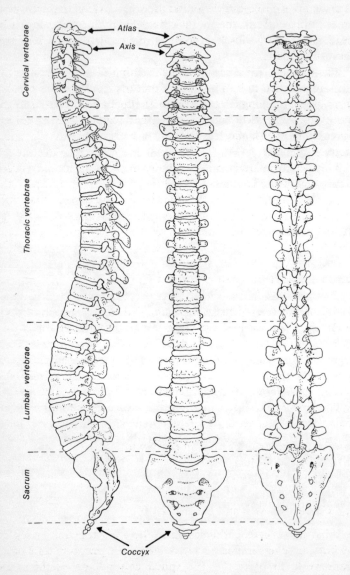

Cervical vertebrae

Atlas

Axis

Thoracic vertebrae

Lumbar vertebrae

Sacrum

Coccyx

Figure 4. The spinal column.

(where the sacrum joins the large pelvic bone), the spinal column is made up of 116 movable joints: there are sixteen in the cervical area, eighty-eight in the thoracic area (including forty-four rib-head and twenty rib-shaft joints), ten lumbar joints and two sacro-iliac joints.

The thoracic spinal region is the least mobile area, because the ribs are attached to it. This means that the spinal nerves passing through the openings in this region are the best protected. In the more mobile cervical and lower lumbar regions, the nerves are much more at risk and it is in these two areas that injuries most frequently occur.

This very brief description excludes many of the more complex structures of the spinal column, but it does give an idea of the importance and complexity of this fantastic piece of engineering. It should also be clear how important it is to good health to maintain its correct function and structural integrity.

The Osteopathic Lesion and Its Causes

Many of the early osteopaths claimed that they achieved their cures by replacing bones that were out of position: the theory was that the 'click' which occurred when they performed a manipulation was caused by a bone going back into place. These days, however, we know that the bones do not jut out of position.

The osteopathic lesion is a general term used in the profession to describe a mechanical disturbance within a joint and its associated structures. Its chief characteristics are as follows:

(a) Restricted or disturbed mobility within a joint
(b) A positional change within a joint
(c) Pain and tenderness
(d) Muscular contraction (spasm)
(e) Changes in skin and tissue texture

What causes osteopathic lesions? The upright posture adopted by human beings imposes a good deal of weight upon the body's framework, in particular the spinal column, pelvis, hips and knees. This renders these joints, together with their associated muscular and connective tissues, particularly susceptible to injuries and disturbances.

While osteopathic lesions can occur in any joint of the body, they occur most commonly in the spine. One reason for this is that the spinal joints are much more complex in structure and motion than the joints of the extremities, like the knee joint, which only has to move backwards and forwards like a hinge. Also, again possibly because of our upright posture, it is far easier for strains and sprains to occur in the spinal muscles, causing muscular spasm, which in turn interferes with normal movement. In addition, during normal everyday activities the spinal joints are not usually called upon to move to their full capacity; then, when they are put through their full range of movement – as in sport or exercise – they are susceptible to strain and injury.

It is not surprising that more and more people are consulting osteopaths for musculoskeletal disturbances, given the modern lifestyle. For example, an increasing number of people are taking up sporting activities. I have come across people taking part in two or three different sports a week, and I have noticed that this has led to an increase in the incidence of sports injury in my practice.

Some sports can be particularly traumatic to the body's framework. Traumas to the body are induced in two ways, either from external impacts to the body (e.g. blows, falls and collisions) or through internal strains, such as sudden twists or excessive stretching. In sports, traumas can arise in both ways. Squash players, for example, frequently suffer shoulder injuries sustained by colliding with the wall of the court in their urgency to hit the ball. There is also the common occurrence of 'pulling' the back while hitting the ball, which usually involves a twisting, bending movement of the trunk. This last happens most frequently for two reasons: firstly, when there is no preparatory warm-up before play, and secondly, when the player becomes overtired. There are other common types or patterns of injury which are specific to particular sports. For example, tennis and golf players frequently get elbow problems – so much so that these have been named 'tennis elbow' and 'golfer's elbow'.

While exercise has its risks, lack of exercise can also put the muscles and joints under stress. Sitting incorrectly and for long periods, slumped over a desk for example, watching television, or driving a car, can all lead to fatigued muscles, stretched ligaments and irritated nerves. Over a period of time, both the structure and function of the areas under strain become chronically disturbed, leading to pain and stiffness in the back and joints.

These disturbances in the human framework are extremely common. If fifty people were taken from the street at random, it is probable that no more than ten per cent would be completely free of an osteopathic lesion somewhere in their bodies.

The Spinal Osteopathic Lesion

This generally consists of a disturbance of mobility between two or more vertebrae. As we have seen, there are twenty-four vertebrae in the spine; these form twenty-four paired joints, each joint having its own set of muscles. The normal spine moves like a flexible rod, with the ability to bend forwards, backwards, sideways and rotationally. All the joints can perform these movements, both singly and in combination – thus you can bend forwards and sideways and, simultaneously, twist. These movements are controlled and governed by the surrounding soft tissues, including the connective tissues, ligaments and small muscle attachments.

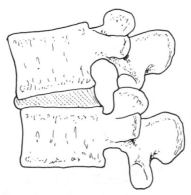

Figure 5. An example of a simple flexion lesion. Here the disc is slightly compressed at its anterior portion. The spinous processes are separated, and movement is restricted in backward-bending.

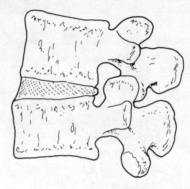

Figure 6. An example of a simple extension lesion. Here the disc is compressed at its posterior portion. The spinous processes are approximated, and movement is restricted in forward-bending.

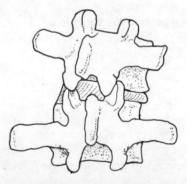

Figure 7. A more complicated lesion, but one that is very frequently detected with osteopathic diagnosis. Here the body of the superior vertebra is held in a position of side-bending and rotation to the right. The disc is seen to be under more compression on the right, and movement is restricted when side-bending and rotation are attempted to the left. In this lesion there is always an involvement of a flexion lesion or extension lesion, as illustrated in Figures 5 and 6.

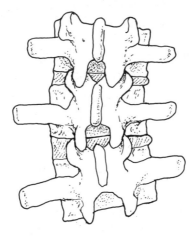

Figure 8. A group lesion, where three or more vertebrae are involved in positional and mobility changes within the spinal joints. Group lesions are usually found in conditions such as scoliosis.

In osteopathy the spine is considered normal when its joints can move through their entire range of motion smoothly and easily, without undue strain to any one joint or its surrounding soft tissues. However, when a spinal joint is considered to be in lesion, its normal functions are impaired: that is, it is restricted in movement and stiff.

In some cases, the joint is not only restricted but has undergone a positional change in that the bones that form the joint are no longer symmetrically placed in relation to each other. The joint is then said to be malaligned. This does not mean that a bone has actually slipped out of place; the malalignment is always within the normal movement capabilities of that joint. For example, when the head is turned to the left, the vertebral joints in the neck have to rotate to the left; but when the head is returned to the neutral position a lesioned joint will not return, and will stay in some degree of rotation, remaining 'fixed' at some point. It is held in this non-neutral position by muscular spasm and tension in the soft tissues. This is because any injury which disturbs the joint must also directly involve the muscles and soft tissues which surround and support it. These tissues, such as the paravertebral muscles that run alongside the spine, together with the tendons and ligaments, are subjected to a considerable amount of tension on at least one side of the lesion. Special nerve endings called proprioceptors are found in the muscles, tendons and joints, which provide information to the brain, via the nervous system, on the degree of tension within our muscles and the position of our joints.

The extra tension caused by a lesion causes these proprioceptors to fire an excessive stream of nerve impulses into the corresponding segment of the spinal cord; their frequency is determined by the severity of the lesion. Because proprioceptors have limited adaptability, this bombardment of nerve impulses is maintained as long as the osteopathic lesion and the tension in the surrounding tissues are maintained. This sustained barrage creates a constant state of excitation, or over-stimulation, at this particular level of the cord, making it easily triggered into activity by additional impulses from any other source.

As a result, there will also be an abnormal discharge of outgoing nerve impulses from this area of the spinal cord to the tissues supplied by these nerves, bringing about changes in the blood flow through various structures and organs, which will show in the skin overlying the tissues as increased moisture, or sweat.

By correcting the osteopathic spinal lesion, a better balance is restored to the central nervous system and in turn to the rest of the bodily tissues involved.

Symptoms of Osteopathic Lesions

While a normal joint is pain-free, there will always be pain or tenderness involved in a spinal osteopathic lesion. When the lesion is acute (i.e. recent), the person is normally aware of some pain at the site. If it continues for some time without being corrected it becomes chronic (i.e. long-standing), and in the later stages the pain may not be noticeable until an osteopath applies controlled pressure to the lesioned area during his examination, which may then locate some tenderness or pain.

When acute lesions are treated simply by rest or pain-killing tablets, the pain may subside, but very often the underlying problem still remains. The lesion then becomes chronic, rendering the area vulnerable. In time, it may possibly become exacerbated after some relatively minor activity, and the original pain and symptoms will return. It is the opinion of most osteopaths that any injury or strain should be examined for the existence of an osteopathic lesion and treated accordingly; immediate treatment of this kind could prevent chronic problems from developing.

While pain and tenderness are usually located at the site of the lesion, they can also be 'remote' or 'referred'. For example, a patient may complain of pain running down the back of the thigh and the outside of the lower leg, with only a vague pain in the lower back. When there are symptoms like this, it is usually a waste of time to try treating the leg, since this is not the real source of the pain. In all probability a joint disturbance will be found in the lower back, in the lumber spine, where the spinal nerve exits. This disturbance causes the referred pain in the leg by irritating some of the nerve fibres that serve and supply the leg-muscles.

Pain is not the only symptom of an osteopathic lesion. The osteopath is trained to look and feel for other signs, including muscle contraction, and the texture of the skin and tissues surrounding the affected joint. It is the combination of all these characteristics that helps him to arrive at a definite diagnosis.

All osteopathic lesions are accompanied by muscle contraction or spasm. These tightened muscles have the effect of splinting the joint, holding it in a position of malalignment which also impairs the normal functions of mobility within the joint. Prolonged muscle contraction slows down the circulatory circuits – the blood vessels involved in carrying metabolic wastes, chiefly lactic acid, away from the muscle. (This is one reason why so many people suffer back-ache in the mornings, which eases or disappears completely once they are up and active: during sleep the blood flow slows down and lactic acid accumulates wherever there is an osteopathic lesion; and activity helps it to disperse.)

As mentioned earlier, in the osteopathic lesion, changes are usually found in the adjacent tissues and overlying skin of the bony segments involved. In the very acute or recent lesion, the osteopath can feel these changes by palpation, that is by using a very light touch with his fingertips, simultaneously stroking his hand down the spine. With this method he will also be able to detect sensations such as an increase in skin temperature, evidence of increased sweating, and perhaps a feeling of bogginess in the tissues, caused by the tissues becoming engorged with excess fluid (oedema). Colour changes may also be seen; usually there is an area of increased redness, and sometimes in an acute lesion, when the osteopath runs his fingers along the spine, the friction creates a red line.

All these signs are evidence of inflammation and are the body's reaction to a recent osteopathic lesion; they are also evidence of disturbance of the autonomic (involuntary) nervous system.

In the chronic lesion, other changes will be detected. To detect these the osteopath uses slightly more pressure in palpation, and the skin and underlying tissues such as the fascia will feel tight and thickened. The skin especially can feel dry, rough and thickened. The superficial muscles and underlying tissues will feel hardened and will reveal a certain ropiness, due to the fibrosis of the tissues – the formation of fibrous tissue or scar tissue, which forms in this case because of a lack of blood supply.

All these features, which can be observed and felt by the trained practitioner, are considerable aids in the diagnosis of the lesion. They can also be very much diminished or totally eliminated by correct treatment.

Types of Osteopathic Lesion

Osteopathy classifies lesions into three basic types: primary, secondary and compensatory.

The Primary Lesion usually consists of a disturbance between two vertebrae. The major cause is trauma, that is the effects of injury caused by an external force like a blow or fall, or by an internal strain such as a twist or sudden stretching movement.

Secondary Lesions normally involve three or more vertebrae, and are commonly called 'group lesions'. Under this classification are found 'reflex lesions'. These are not produced by injury, but are the result of irritation within the internal organs such as the heart, gall-bladder and kidneys. Figure 9 shows how a kind of cycle occurs. A diseased or irritated organ relays an abnormal rate of nerve impulses back to the spinal cord at the level related to that organ, and thence to the muscles around the spinal joints. This causes the muscles to contract, with associated tenderness over the related joints.

Osteopaths believe that the process can also occur in reverse: that is, a primary lesion can reflexly disturb the function of an internal organ by sending abnormal nerve impulses to that organ.

Compensatory Lesions, as the term implies, arise through the body's efforts to compensate for other lesions. If a joint becomes fixed and loses its normal mobility as a result of a primary lesion, the joints above and below sometimes try to compensate for this restriction by becoming hyper-mobile; that is, they adopt too great a range of movement, which makes them become weak and unstable. This condition has to be treated differently from the normal joint restriction; as certain types of manipulative thrusting techniques could further stretch and strain the already unstable joint, more gentle methods will be required.

The Mimicking Effects of Osteopathic Lesions

As we have seen, on some occasions the area where the patient experiences pain may suggest that some functional disturbance of an inner organ is reflecting back to the related vertebrae. Conversely, symptoms produced by osteopathic lesions can mimic visceral (inner organ) and other disorders. Lesions found in the upper neck, for instance, may produce symptoms of giddiness similar to the condition known as Ménière's disease.

If a patient complains, for example, of pain in the upper chest area, across the upper shoulder and running down the inside of the left arm, the osteopath might at first suspect that he has a

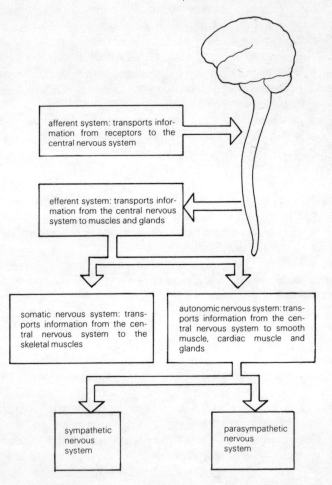

The central nervous system is made up of the brain and the spinal cord

afferent system: transports information from receptors to the central nervous system

efferent system: transports information from the central nervous system to muscles and glands

somatic nervous system: transports information from the central nervous system to the skeletal muscles

autonomic nervous system: transports information from the central nervous system to smooth muscle, cardiac muscle and glands

sympathetic nervous system

parasympathetic nervous system

The peripheral nervous system is made up of the afferent, efferent, somatic, autonomic, sympathetic and parasympathetic nervous systems

Figure 9. The central and peripheral nervous systems.

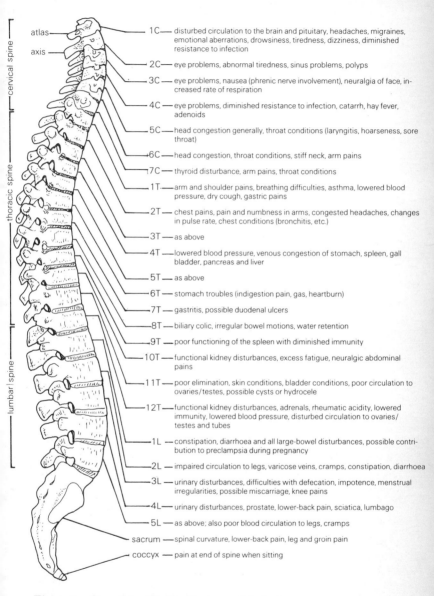

atlas
axis

cervical spine
thoracic spine
lumbar spine

1C — disturbed circulation to the brain and pituitary, headaches, migraines, emotional aberrations, drowsiness, tiredness, dizziness, diminished resistance to infection

2C — eye problems, abnormal tiredness, sinus problems, polyps

3C — eye problems, nausea (phrenic nerve involvement), neuralgia of face, increased rate of respiration

4C — eye problems, diminished resistance to infection, catarrh, hay fever, adenoids

5C — head congestion generally, throat conditions (laryngitis, hoarseness, sore throat)

6C — head congestion, throat conditions, stiff neck, arm pains

7C — thyroid disturbance, arm pains, throat conditions

1T — arm and shoulder pains, breathing difficulties, asthma, lowered blood pressure, dry cough, gastric pains

2T — chest pains, pain and numbness in arms, congested headaches, changes in pulse rate, chest conditions (bronchitis, etc.)

3T — as above

4T — lowered blood pressure, venous congestion of stomach, spleen, gall bladder, pancreas and liver

5T — as above

6T — stomach troubles (indigestion pain, gas, heartburn)

7T — gastritis, possible duodenal ulcers

8T — biliary colic, irregular bowel motions, water retention

9T — poor functioning of the spleen with diminished immunity

10T — functional kidney disturbances, excess fatigue, neuralgic abdominal pains

11T — poor elimination, skin conditions, bladder conditions, poor circulation to ovaries/testes, possible cysts or hydrocele

12T — functional kidney disturbances, adrenals, rheumatic acidity, lowered immunity, lowered blood pressure, disturbed circulation to ovaries/testes and tubes

1L — constipation, diarrhoea and all large-bowel disturbances, possible contribution to preclampsia during pregnancy

2L — impaired circulation to legs, varicose veins, cramps, constipation, diarrhoea

3L — urinary disturbances, difficulties with defecation, impotence, menstrual irregularities, possible miscarriage, knee pains

4L — urinary disturbances, prostate, lower-back pain, sciatica, lumbago

5L — as above; also poor blood circulation to legs, cramps

sacrum — spinal curvature, lower-back pain, leg and groin pain

coccyx — pain at end of spine when sitting

Figure 10. Possible effects of osteopathic lesions.

heart problem. No reputable osteopath would claim to cure heart disease, and in such a case it is of the utmost importance that the patient be given a correct diagnosis before any treatment is given. However, many people suffering with these symptoms have already had extensive medical examinations and have been told that there is nothing organically wrong with their hearts. In these cases the osteopath can often help, by finding and correcting the problems in the spine and rib cage that are causing the symptoms that *mimic* a heart disorder.

Lesions of the lower neck and upper trunk (the thoracic spine) can mimic heart pain, similar to the pain caused by angina. Pain coming from lesions existing in the mid-thoracic spine (between the shoulder blades) can also simulate a peptic ulcer. Pain from rib lesions can sometimes be wrongly identified as pleurisy or some other disorder of an organ. Lesions in the lower back and pelvic joints can cause pain similar to most of the gynaecological diseases.

Osteopaths, therefore, have to be concerned with much more than bones: they need to be aware of all aspects of bodily health and have a thorough knowledge of anatomy and physiology. The knowledge that osteopathic lesions can mimic other disorders is extremely important in the correct management and treatment of the patient. It is equally important for the osteopath to know that visceral disease can produce symptoms similar to osteopathic lesions. It would be wrong for the osteopath to treat pain in the lower back caused by a gynaecological disorder, just as it is wrong for the doctor to prescribe antacids for pain resembling a peptic ulcer, when the actual cause of the pain is a mid-thoracic spinal lesion.

CASE HISTORY

A twenty-nine-year-old man consulted me for pains in his left shoulder area, between his shoulder blade and spine. This became worse on exertion, when the pains radiated into his left chest area and down his left arm. He also complained of breathlessness and light-headedness when he walked any distance, and he had had to give up his sporting activities of karate and golf.

When he came to see me the symptoms had been troubling

him for about eight months with no apparent improvement. His doctor had sent him to hospital for an electrocardiogram, which revealed nothing abnormal about his heart. X-rays of his cervical spine also showed no abnormality. After these examinations he was told that his problem was muscular, and he was prescribed some physiotherapy, consisting mainly of electrical treatments. These brought about temporary relief, but his symptoms always returned after a short time. During our consultation he mentioned that his pains seemed to have started after he had visited the golf range; on becoming tired during his practice swings, he had accidentally hit the ground very hard with the golf club. Afterwards he had felt a sharp pain, but as it subsided after a couple of days, he had not considered the incident to be very important.

On examining him, I found a primary lesion at the second thoracic vertebra, which was also affecting the second rib where it joins up with this vertebra. (These joints are known as the costovertebral joints.) Further examination of the ribs on the left side revealed that, when he breathed in, there was a restriction in the movement of his second to fifth ribs. This condition, commonly found in osteopathic examination procedures, affects the muscles attached to these ribs, preventing them from contracting enough to take in a full in-breath.

Various osteopathic manipulations were used to restore correct mobility and joint alignment within the involved spinal joint and ribs. I treated the second thoracic vertebra by using a direct thrust to the joint. The rib problem required a different manipulative approach called 'muscular energy technique', described more fully in Chapter 5.

After his first visit there was a vast improvement in the patient's symptoms, and after three further treatments he was free both of pain and of the osteopathic lesions that had caused his symptoms.

CHAPTER FOUR

VISITING

AN OSTEOPATH

When a patient first visits an osteopath it is normally upon the recommendation of a friend, relative or acquaintance, or even – increasingly often these days – the patient's doctor. Most osteopaths run an appointment system; an average visit lasts between thirty and forty minutes. Charges vary from practitioner to practitioner, ranging between eight and twenty-five pounds, some osteopaths charging more for the initial visit and consultation.

The Consultation

Most osteopaths, myself included, consider that the consultation and history-taking is just as important as the clinical examination that follows, as they will guide the osteopath towards the diagnosis upon which he will base his treatment. Patients are sometimes surprised by this; people who consult osteopaths are usually in pain and, understandably, their prime concern is to be relieved of discomfort as quickly as possible. I remember a man calling at my practice without an appointment, wanting to be seen there and then. My receptionist explained that I was already attending to a patient, and asked if he could call back later in the day, when he could be seen. He replied that while they were standing about talking, the osteopath could have 'popped' his bones back! Like many people, he clearly had no idea that before any treatment could be given, the osteopath has to make a thorough examination leading to a clinical diagnosis. At times, indeed, only a tentative diagnosis can be made at this point, which must be confirmed and aided by X-rays and/or laboratory tests.

The purpose of the consultation is for the osteopath to obtain as much information as possible about the patient's present condition, general health and past medical history. The good osteopath makes sure that this takes place in a friendly and relaxed atmosphere; most people on their first visit are apprehensive, nervous and tense, and it is the practitioner's job to put them at their ease and gain their confidence. I believe that confidence in the therapist is a very important contributory factor in the effectiveness of the treatment as a whole. If a patient has no faith in a practitioner, of whatever therapy, progress is likely to be slow, and the treatment unlikely to achieve the best results. This is not to suggest that osteopathy depends on faith alone; far from it. It is a physical form of treatment, requiring knowledge and skill.

At this first visit, the osteopath takes a case history, starting by ascertaining the patient's presenting symptoms – the symptoms from which he is currently suffering. Once these are established, the patient will be asked about his or her past medical history and general health. Most osteopaths, incidentally, prefer to hold the consultation with the patient alone; sometimes wives, friends or relatives like to be present, but they can be over-helpful in answering questions on the patient's behalf! Only the person who is suffering the pain can describe their symptoms and explain how they feel. My one exception to this rule is in the case of children, who can always be accompanied by a parent or guardian.

What sort of questions does the osteopath ask? Let us suppose you are consulting him for a spinal pain in the lower back, a very common complaint. He will want to know how long you have had the pain, and whether it was caused by an injury or started for no apparent reason. He will ask what type of pain it is – whether it is sharp, or more of a dull ache, whether it is constant or intermittent. He will want to know whether the pain is getting worse or remaining the same, what aggravates it and what eases it, whether you would describe it as severe, moderate or mild, and whether it refers to any other area, such as the legs, groin or abdomen. The answers to all these questions provide detailed information about the causes of your symptoms, and the osteopath will continue to ask you to describe your pain until he is satisfied that he has obtained all the information he needs.

Next, he will ask whether your general health is satisfactory or whether you are aware of any other health problems, whether you have suffered from any serious illnesses in the past, and what medication, if any, you have been prescribed; he will make specific notes of the names of any drugs you may be taking. These questions are important in formulating a picture of your general health. They will help the osteopath to know whether your pain is mechanical in origin, or if there is an existing health problem which relates to it, and, if so, whether the pain is possibly contributing to the health problem. He will be very interested in any previous history of back trouble, including accidents, injuries or heavy falls, no matter how long ago. He will also ask about any treatment you have received for the complaint, how effective it was, and whether any X-rays or laboratory tests have been undertaken, together with their results.

During the consultation, the osteopath will be employing his listening skills to the full. He not only needs an accurate record of the symptoms; he can also gain valuable information about the patient's personality and reaction to their pain from their tone of voice. People who have suffered pain for a long time, and may have already consulted other osteopaths or therapists without relief, are often depressed about their situation. They will tend to give rather negative responses to questions and conversation, indicating that although they are still hoping for help they have become somewhat despondent. With patients like these, it is important that the practitioner himself adopts a very positive approach, and gains the patient's confidence whenever possible. A good osteopath will do this by giving a very thorough consultation and examination, explaining fully and clearly what he finds, and reassuring the patient that he can be helped. He should be careful, however, not to give false hope in any condition which may be beyond the scope of, or unsuitable for, osteopathic treatment.

For example, he will note any speech impediment, in particular slow responses to questions, and hesitancy or difficulty in remembering words; these may indicate that there are neurological problems, such as multiple sclerosis, Friedrich's ataxia, or possibly a brain tumour or some disturbance of the circulation of the brain, like a stroke. In such cases he will immediately refer the patient for specialist treatment.

By the end of the consultation the osteopath should have a good idea as to whether osteopathic treatment is suitable. From his findings, he may decide that the patient should return to his doctor, or possibly see some other alternative practitioner who may be better suited to his needs. Of course, on some occasions, this cannot be decided until after he has made a detailed examination.

The Osteopathic Examination

This falls basically into three parts: a general examination, specific localized examination, and special tests that may be required for certain cases. In working towards a diagnosis, the osteopath uses a number of skills including listening, observation, palpation, and his knowledge of the related structures and physiology of the patient's pain syndrome.

The Physical Examination consists first of simply looking at the patient. The osteopath will observe the contours of the body, noting any obvious distortions in spinal alignment and posture. Standing behind the patient, he will start from the head and work downwards. First, he will note whether the head is sitting straight or tilted to one side; he will look at the posterior muscles of the neck, and note any signs of contraction and strain. He will place his hands on the tips of the patient's shoulders to check whether they are level or whether one side is higher than the other; he will compare this measurement with the lower slopes of the shoulder blades, noting whether there is an equal distance between each shoulder blade and the spine. Working further downwards, he will look at the level of the pelvic crests (the top of the pelvic bones), noting any distortion, twist or difference in their relative heights. He will check the levels of the superior edges of the greater trochanters of the hips (at the top of the hip bones where they join the pelvic bones), and will also feel for any contractions in the muscles down the thighs and calves. On reaching the feet he will check the arches by placing an index finger under each – he won't be able to do this if the feet are flat, and flat feet can cause pelvic and spinal problems, particularly if one arch is worse than the other. (Good feet and arches act as efficient shock absorbers for the rest of the weight-bearing joints; the ankles, knees, hips, pelvic and spinal joints.)

The practitioner will then look at the patient from the side, making similar observations from head to toe. During this whole visual examination he will be recording his findings, making a note of any abnormal spinal curvatures he finds. These abnormal contours are indications of muscular imbalances and possible spinal mechanical problems – osteopathic lesions of either primary or secondary origin.

The next step is to examine the patient's gait, noting whether this is normal or whether there is a limp, which could denote a hip problem, painful sciatica, or even a mechanical problem within the pelvis, among other things. The osteopath will go on to test the general mobility of the spine, by asking the patient to bend forwards, backwards and sideways and to rotate the trunk. While the patient is performing these movements, the osteopath will note any restrictions or lack of mobility in the spinal column. For example, when the patient turns his head to left and right, any restricted movement on either side will be clearly seen, indicating possible lesions in the neck. Or when the patient bends forward, the osteopath may observe a 'flattening' of certain areas due to restriction, or more muscle mass on one side, denoting a possible rotational curvature of the spine in this area.

All these distortions and restrictions of motion can be caused by osteopathic lesions. The osteopath will next go on to make a more detailed examination of these areas by palpation and motion-testing procedures.

Palpation is defined in *Butterworth's Medical Dictionary* as 'a method of physical examination in which the hands are applied to the surface of the body, so that by the sense of touch, information is obtained about the condition of the skin, the underlying tissues and organs'. The art of palpation is probably the most important clinical diagnostic tool the osteopath has. Many are so proficient in this tactile art that they can feel and pick up the most minute and subtle changes in texture, temperature, tissue reaction and joint mobility. One very famous American osteopath, the late William Garner Sutherland, put it well when he said that the skilful osteopath could think, feel and see with his ten little fingers.

The osteopath uses these ten fingers to detect all the characteristics of the osteopathic lesion. They can tell him whether the lesion is acute, sub-acute or chronic, which is important, as the treatment approach will normally be different for the acute stage and the chronic stage. He will palpate the joints involved, both in a static state and in motion.

Figure 11. Palpatory and mobility testing for tension and restriction of spinal areas.

Mobility-testing Procedures are used to obtain information while the joint is in motion. The osteopath will ask the patient to relax while he himself puts the joints through their normal physiological range of movements, comparing their function and mobility with those of the joints above and below. A normal joint will be able to move through its natural range of movement without any strain on the surrounding tissues; the movement will feel easy to the operator and painless to the patient.

For example, to examine the spine between the shoulder blades, the area known as the mid-thoracic spine, the osteopath will ask the patient to sit in a relaxed position; then with one hand he will bend the patient's trunk forwards, backwards, in rotation and sideways in a slow rhythmical manner. With the other hand, he will feel whether the spinal segments and tissues in this area are moving smoothly and easily as they should, or whether they are binding and reacting against the movements. Where there is no lesion or pathology, the spine will perform these movements easily and freely, with no pain or muscular contraction. An abnormal, lesioned joint may feel restricted in certain movement patterns, and the surrounding tissues will react against these movements; this tissue reaction can easily be felt by the osteopath as a tightening and binding of the tissues as well as a binding of the joint itself. He will go on to perform a similar motion-palpatory examination of any other areas of the spine that may be under suspicion, and possibly other joints such as the knees and feet.

The osteopath will not perform any kind of manipulative technique until he has carried out all these examination procedures, and has ascertained which joints are causing the pain – there is no point in manipulating a normal movable joint.

Clinical Tests. As has already been mentioned, the osteopath examines not just the obvious trouble spots, but also the body as a whole, looking for structural mechanical problems that may interfere with bodily functioning. It may be that his findings lead him to suspect that the patient's problem is outside the field of osteopathy. In this case he will use clinical tests to confirm his observations. These range from testing the reflexes (such as the triceps, biceps, patella and achilles) by tapping the tendon areas for reflex response, to the 'Babinksi' test, which is performed by slowly stroking the sole of the foot to check for neurological disease. Another test is to see whether there are differences in sensation in some parts of the body; these can be evaluated by pricking lightly with a pin, stroking, or determining whether the patient can feel the difference between heat and cold. Lack of sensation may indicate that there is some interruption of the spinal nerves that supply the related areas of the skin.

The blood pressure and pulse are frequently taken, too, to provide basic information about the cardiovascular system. Auscultation (listening with a stethoscope) may also be performed to assess the state of the heart and lungs.

If it becomes obvious as a result of these tests, or at any stage of the consultation, that the patient's condition is not a structural mechanical problem, the osteopath will always advise the patient to consult his doctor. For example, a young lady once visited my practice on the recommendation of her mother, who was already a patient of mine; she was suffering pain in the area of her ribs, radiating round to the right side of her thoracic spine. I found that her general bodily temperature was very high, and when I listened to her lungs I could hear an abnormally high 'thrill' sound, a noise which I thought was probably caused by friction of the pleura, that is, the swollen membranes of the lungs rubbing against each other. All the signs and symptoms indicated that she was suffering from pleurisy, and I immediately referred her to her doctor, who confirmed my diagnosis.

Sometimes referral works both ways, with doctors referring patients to osteopaths. This can be very helpful, particularly when the doctor has already referred the patient for X-rays or laboratory tests, and is willing to inform the osteopath of their results. For example, this extra knowledge may aid the osteopath in ruling out pathological complications such as an active in-flammatory arthritis, which would contra-indicate specific joint manipulation. Cooperation between doctors and osteopaths can only be of benefit to such patients; it is a great pity when there is no communication between the two professions.

Contra-indications. It is important for the osteopath to establish whether the patient is suffering from any condition which would contra-indicate some or all of his manipulative techniques, and he has some specific tests for this purpose. If they prove positive, this is usually because there is some underlying pathological problem, such as a weakening of the bone tissue, or spinal cord or nerve pressure. There may be anatomical abnormalities, or even disturbances of the circulatory systems, such as arteriosclerosis (hardening of the arteries). All of these are conditions for which harsh or wrongly employed manipulation could be damaging.

For example, before manipulating the neck region, a simple test is to have the patient sitting or lying on his back with his head extending beyond the couch. The osteopath then slowly bends his head backwards, and then side-bends and rotates it to one side. If this produces any symptoms of dizziness, or any evidence of the eyes rolling up, down or from side to side, these would be definite indications not to perform any manipulation without further investigation. Another frequently used test for the neck is known as the 'flexion test'. The patient lies on his back, and the osteopath raises his head so that the chin is carried towards the chest. If this test produces pins and needles (paraesthesia) in the arms and legs, cervical manipulation should not be carried out; it is usually a sign that there is pressure on or towards the spinal cord.

In nine years of practice I have only come across one such case, but this simple test, which only takes a few seconds, prevented me from manipulating the neck. The patient was a girl of fifteen who had fallen off her horse on to the top of her head, buckling her neck awkwardly. She complained of pain and stiffness in her neck, and pins and needles in both hands. Although osteopaths use the tests described in a routine manner, the symptoms of pins and needles in both hands when carrying out certain neck movements would in any case arouse suspicion. When I performed the flexion test, she not only complained of an increase in the pins and needles in her hands but also felt them in her feet. I immediately referred her to an orthopaedic surgeon, who found a large disc protrusion between the fifth and sixth cervical joints of the neck. The increased symptoms during the neck flexion test showed that the protrusion was severe enough to press on the spinal cord, and any forceful manipulation to the neck could have had serious consequences.

In the lower back, symptoms such as loss of bladder or bowel control would be a definite contra-indication to manipulation, as they can indicate serious neurological pressure on the tail of the spinal cord known as the *cauda equina*. In this area the osteopath can use simple compression tests of the pelvis to gain information about the sacro-iliac joints. If these cause pain, this may indicate that the sacro-iliac joints are hyper-mobile, making it unwise to use thrusting types of manipulation. This test may also indicate that these joints are undergoing inflammatory changes such as those caused by active rheumatoid arthritis, in which case, again, manipulation would be very unwise.

In some cases, even when these tests prove positive, the osteopath can still employ some of the very gentle manipulative techniques that have been developed over the years, using the minimum of force. Such techniques make osteopathy a very safe and efficient form of treatment.

X-rays. It is not always necessary for a patient to have a radiological examination before treatment. Many of the problems confronting the osteopath are straightforward musculoskeletal joint dysfunctions brought about by sporting or occupational activities, or by heavy lifting, where there is a definite history of a strain or injury having taken place, with the patient knowing exactly when the trouble started. However, X-rays are necessary when the practitioner suspects that some other pathology may be causing the patient's pain.

There are specific indications for an X-ray examination. One is when a patient presents with chronic pain, has responded poorly to previous treatment, osteopathic or otherwise, and has nct so far had an X-ray examination. Another is when gentle treatment provokes an over-reaction in the patient out of proportion to the presenting symptoms; gentle treatment should not worsen the condition unless there is some acute pathological condition causing the patient's general resistance to be very low. Finally, if the patient's general health picture is not good, especially if there has already been surgical intervention to remove some tissue growth in the past, the osteopath will want an up-to-date X-ray, and possibly other laboratory tests, before giving any treatment.

Should the osteopath decide that X-rays are needed, he normally has three options: his own X-ray facilities, referral to a doctor, or referral to a private radiologist. It is rare, however, for osteopaths to have their own X-ray facilities. Although they are ideal for making on-the-spot examinations and diagnoses, there are drawbacks, since the strict safety regulations require essential precautions such as lead-lined walls.

There are also drawbacks to referring the patient back to his doctor, with a recommendation of the type of X-ray investigation needed. If the doctor agrees, the osteopath can obtain a report of the investigation; however, on most occasions the osteopath does not see the actual X-ray. Even when no abnormality of serious bone pathology is reported, it could be useful for the osteopath to see whether the X-ray itself shows up any problems related to the patient's symptoms from the osteopathic point of view which may not appear in the report. For example, it might show an abnormality in the curvature of the spine; any straightening within the natural curve can point to mechanical problems, indicating osteopathic lesions. It can also allow him to study the facets of the spinal joints (the linkages of the intervertebral bone segments); there are sometimes variations in their symmetry which require a specific manipulative approach. A scoliosis finding on an X-ray may be omitted from the radiologist's report because it is not considered relevant to the patient's presenting condition; but to the osteopath, provided the X-ray was taken with the patient standing, it could indicate an anatomical short leg or a sacral base tilt due to lesioning of the sacro-iliac joints, either of which could cause a lateral scoliotic curve.

This last observation could be important, since correcting this type of malalignment of the sacral base can eliminate symptoms not obviously related to this area, such as headaches. This is because the tension produced by this fault in the musculoskeletal system can lead to mechanical problems as high up as the neck.

The third option is for the practitioner to advise his patient to have X-rays taken privately. Although this involves the patient in additional expense, I feel that it is worthwhile, since it enables the osteopath to obtain the X-ray pictures to study as well as a report by a radiologist with specialist training in reading bone pathologies and structural abnormalities. In England two institutions offer this service: Cavendish X-rays and the X-ray department of the British School of Osteopathy. Unfortunately both are in London, and travel can present problems for patients who are in extreme pain. It is a great pity that osteopaths do not have the right to send their patients to their local hospital for X-rays, or to obtain a sight of the X-rays as well as a report.

Few osteopaths feel that an X-ray investigation should be undertaken as a matter of routine prior to treatment. On most occasions, once the consultation and examination have been made, some treatment can be given on the initial visit. The success of this and subsequent treatments will of course depend heavily on the accuracy of the osteopath's diagnosis.

CASE HISTORY

The following story will give you an idea of the importance of the consultation and examination.

Mrs D, a woman of sixty, came to see me complaining of pain in her right leg which had started the week before for no apparent reason. She also told me that she had been suffering with bronchitis and a bad cough. I could see from her general appearance that she was not in robust health, and when we talked she confirmed this; she was suffering from constipation, haemorrhoids, rheumatism and a hiatus hernia. She had previously received osteopathic treatment from a colleague for low-back pain and sciatica, and she described the pain in her leg as similar to this sciatic pain, but without the low-back pain which had accompanied it in the past.

After completing the consultation, I came to the conclusion that this was not a typical sciatic pain, but possibly a thrombosis in the leg concerned. Physical examination further confirmed my diagnosis, although clinically I could not tell if it was an arterial or deep-vein thrombosis. I was concerned because she had had the condition for at least a week, and recommended her to consult her doctor immediately. There was nothing I could do for her, since osteopathic treatment would have been detrimental to her health. She did see her doctor and was admitted to hospital the same day, where she received the appropriate medical attention.

Treatment

Once he has made his diagnosis, the osteopath may well be able to start treatment during the first visit. Patients usually want to know how many treatments they will need: this of course varies according to the type of problem, how long-standing it is, and the patient's age. Generally, there could be signs of improvement in a long-standing condition within about six visits. The more simple strain or recent osteopathic lesion may need only a few treatments. Osteopaths are careful not to over-treat, preferring to rely on the body's inherent self-healing mechanisms and stimulating these with osteopathic treatment when needed.

The frequency of treatments must again depend on the type of problem involved. An acute problem may need two visits in one week, whereas a sub-acute or more chronic condition may require only one visit a week. Once the condition has been brought under control, periodic visits may be needed to maintain this improvement.

People often ask if manipulations are painful to receive. Generally they should not be, since a good osteopath only uses the minimum of force to achieve the desired result. The various types of osteopathic manipulation are described in the next chapter, and as will be seen, many of them are extremely gentle. Many of my patients tell me how much they enjoy the treatment and say they find it very relaxing. Sometimes a little soreness or exacerbation of the pain is experienced after a treatment, not unlike the muscle ache experienced after a physical work-out or the first stint in the garden. Usually this occurs in people suffering with more chronic problems, and it generally only lasts a few days.

CHAPTER FIVE

OSTEOPATHIC TECHNIQUES

When I say that the osteopath considers the whole person in his diagnosis and treatment, I do not mean that he cracks every joint in the patient's body – far from it. However, part of his job is to search the whole body for osteopathic lesions and eliminate those he discovers. This helps to restore structural integrity and function, giving the whole body an opportunity to achieve health and harmony. Of prime importance, too – and probably more important initially to the patient – is the practitioner's ability to relieve pain as quickly and efficiently as possible.

To achieve this, the osteopath concentrates on the musculoskeletal system. His training will have equipped him with a wide range of techniques, technically referred to as the osteopathic armamentarium, from which he will select the most suitable for each particular case. If a patient presents with multiple areas of dysfunction, these may not all be treated in one session. There is a risk of over-treating the body, which can cause unnecessary short-term reactions, such as soreness and aching, similar to the after-effects of unaccustomed exercise. Instead, the osteopath will give several treatments, focusing chiefly on the primary problems first; then, if any secondary problems still remain, he will go on to deal with these.

Good osteopathic treatment is *specific* for each individual patient: that is, manipulative techniques are selected to be applied to specific disorders in a particular person's musculoskeletal framework. Some types of manipulative therapists give a generalized treatment to all-comers, using the same techniques every time. Such routine procedures have no place in osteopathy. Although they may sometimes be successful, this is usually the result of good luck rather than good judgement. Another defect of the generalized approach is that when a patient reports that the pain is easier, the practitioner has no idea which particular technique, applied to which part of the body, has been responsible for the improvement.

With specific treatment, each individual's pattern of joint dysfunction is recorded, so that a careful and accurate assessment can be made of their progress at each visit. When the patient reports considerable alleviation of their pain, the osteopath will know which of his specific techniques has brought about this improvement. He can then re-check the areas of dysfunction to assess whether he has completely eliminated the lesion, or whether there is still some evidence of the derangement. In such cases, further treatment may be needed to reduce the possibility of a recurrence, should the area undergo minimal stress or strain.

When selecting a technique, the osteopath considers his own physical build and ability in relation to the patient's age, size, general health, muscular tone and strength. He aims to use the minimum of force, applying the technique with correct timing and precision of leverage. I know of a fellow osteopath who is only four feet ten inches tall and weighs no more than seven stone; yet the skilful use of precise techniques enables her to manipulate people three times her size.

Many people are still under the impression that for a manipulation to be successful the osteopath has to obtain an audible crack or click from the joints. This is not necessarily true. Many of the techniques used in osteopathic manipulative therapy are devised to release contractions in the muscles and soft tissues, which will reduce pain and help to restore normal mobility and alignment in the strained joint. Although these particular techniques are very gentle, producing no audible 'cracks', they can be extremely effective and should not be underestimated.

During their training, student osteopaths spend many hours practising the range of manipulative techniques, first on each other and then on patients in clinics, under supervision. This practice equips them to apply the correct procedure in all the different clinical situations they may meet with in their professional life, and to modify them to suit each patient's needs. It is here that osteopathy truly becomes an art. While a thorough training is important there is no doubt that some people are more gifted than others, and are possessed of some innate ability in applying their skills.

The osteopathic armamentarium of techniques can be broken down into three main headings: soft-tissue manipulation, passive motion techniques (known in the profession as articulatory techniques) and specific joint manipulation.

Soft-tissue Manipulation

This consists of massage-type movements designed to treat the muscles, ligaments and fascial (connective) tissues. They include stroking, kneading, friction and stretching, using various degrees of pressure from light to deep. They are used for specific purposes, either to relax or to stimulate the tissues.

Soft-tissue manipulation normally precedes the manipulation of any joint, and as well as having a beneficial effect on the tissues it can aid the osteopath in his diagnosis. While working on the soft tissues he may pick up sensations of muscular contraction or thickening and ropiness (sometimes referred to as fibrositis), which indicate that the tissues have undergone chemical changes normally related to a chronic, or long-standing osteopathic lesion. Areas like this are given specific attention with soft-tissue manipulation in order to break down the ropiness and thickness.

Another advantage of using soft-tissue manipulation before specific joint correction is that it not only relaxes localized tissue contractions, but also 'de-tenses' the patient as a whole. When carried out in a quiet, relaxed manner it can be very soothing – and a relaxed patient finds it easier to cooperate with the osteopath during the techniques that follow, whereas tense patients often unconsciously resist specific joint corrections. (While on the subject of relaxation, orthopaedic surgeons often give their patients a general anaesthetic before manipulating them. I feel there are some disadvantages to this, for which see page 22.)

Within the category of soft-tissue manipulation, osteopaths employ several types of technique.

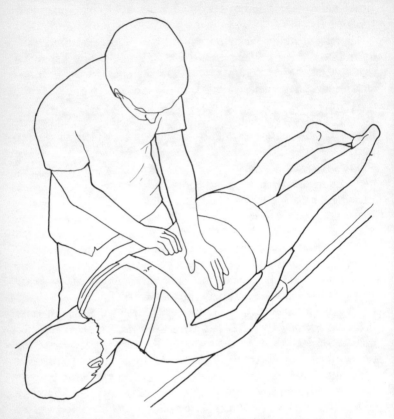

Figure 12. The osteopath performing soft-tissue manipulation, pushing the muscle mass away from the spinous processes in a rhythmical manner in order to relax and reduce tightness and spasm of the muscles.

Effleurage, stroking the tissues, is good for effecting lymphatic and venous (vein) drainage. It can be performed in a light or deep manner, using the fingertips or palms in a sweeping, flowing fashion, always working towards the heart. This type of movement can also benefit cases of acute trauma that have caused a lot of swelling to a joint such as the knee by aiding drainage of the engorged tissues.

Frictional Movements are performed in small, circular or to-and-fro movements of the thumbs or fingers over muscles, tendons and ligaments. Ligaments are much lower in blood supply than muscular tissue, and normally take longer to heal. Frictional massage produces a toning effect and promotes increased blood supply, thus promoting faster healing.

Kneading Movements also help to stimulate the tissues by improving the circulation to the muscles and areas involved. In particular, kneading the upper trapezius muscles across the shoulders relieves fibrous contractions and tension, which can be most soothing and beneficial for the patient.

Stretching Manoeuvres can also be used for muscle relaxation; combined with slow, rhythmical rocking movements they can reduce congestion and improve the circulation of the lymph and blood. When applying these to the neck, the osteopath will use one hand to stabilize the shoulder girdle while the other slowly stretches the head and neck away from the shoulder.

To stretch the muscular tissues of the lower back, one method is to have the patient lying on his side with the operator's forearm resting against the pelvis and the other forearm resting on the lower ribs, with his hands contacting the mass of the *erector spinae*, the large muscles running up the back. By separating the forearms and pulling up on the muscles, the osteopath creates a powerful but controlled stretch in the base of the lower back. This helps to relieve the spasm that occurs in many painful lower backs.

Osteopathic stretching techniques are also useful in releasing the intercostal muscles, which lie between each rib, together with the muscle of the diaphragm, thus enabling the patient to breathe more deeply.

Inhibitory Treatment is the name given to slowly applied massage-type techniques aimed at relaxing and reducing muscle spasm, and easing pain. Pressure is applied to the muscles in specific ways in a slow and rhythmical manner until a release in the muscle spasm and tension is achieved and the pressure is slowly

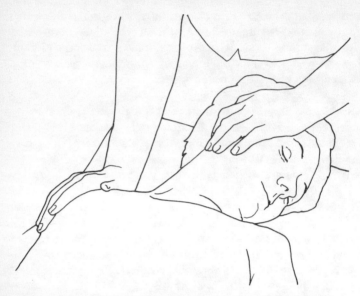

Figure 13. The osteopath slowly stretches the head and neck away from the stabilized shoulder. This gently stretches the muscles and improves venous and lymphatic drainage.

reduced. For example, inhibition of the muscles and tissues of the neck can be performed in various ways. A common and efficient method is to have the patient lying comfortably on their back. The osteopath stands to the side and places one hand on the forehead, steadying it while he reaches across the tissues of the neck with the other hand and gently and rhythmically pulls these tissues towards him until the tension is released.

Inhibitory pressures may be used to reduce the muscular pain and spasm in the lower back known to many people as 'lumbago'. The osteopath asks the patient to lie face down; then, standing at one side, he gently and rhythmically pushes the muscle mass away from the spinous processes, the central joints of the spine. Sometimes, when the lower back muscles are in acute severe spasm, it may not be beneficial for the patient to be face down; in this case the osteopath will adapt by having the patient lie on one side with the legs semi-flexed for comfort. From this position, the osteopath relaxes the musculature by pulling the tissues up and towards himself, continuing with this rhythmical inhibitory pressure until he can feel a sense of release in the tissues.

Neuro-muscular Massage Technique

This is a very deep form of massage technique which is not used by all osteopaths. It is normally used to balance and tone the muscular system, ligaments and connective tissue. It is believed that the muscles surrounding the spine act like the guy-ropes of a tent-pole, helping to keep it erect. Before using the technique, the osteopath will make a diagnosis to detect the soft-tissue lesions that are involved with spinal lesions. Treating these areas, generally by performing a stripping motion with the thumbs, or even with the fleshy part of the forearm near the elbow, along the muscles enables tight muscles and tissues to relax and release. Osteopaths who employ this method believe that it makes the subsequent specific joint manipulation easier to accomplish.

Chapman's Neuro-lymphatic Reflex Points

These are very small nodules found under the surface of the skin along the back and front of the body. Technically, they are discribed as small areas of gangliform contractions of lymphoid tissue, and they are found in the lymphoid tissue at the outer ends of the spinal nerves. They can become over-congested through physical injury, infection, degeneration or chemical irritation.

Treating them can bring about good results in a variety of conditions, including headaches, sinusitis, conjunctivitis, poor circulation in the arms and legs, bronchitis, constipation, indigestion, and some types of sciatic pain, to name just a few! Not all osteopaths include them in their treatment, but I personally have found them both interesting and rewarding in relation to some of my patients' problems.

The points were found by an American osteopath, Frank Chapman, who studied at the first osteopathic school, the American School of Osteopathy. He spent much time studying and researching them in a clinical environment, and the points became known within the profession as 'Chapman's reflexes' in re-cognition of his work. The term 'reflex' was used because Chapman believed that a lymphatic congestion in an organ produces an irritation which in turn causes a response of abnormal stimulus in certain nerve fibres – that is to say, the congestion in the organ is *reflected* in the nervous system. One of the basic functions of the lymphatic system is to act like a sewage system, filtering many foreign and potentially harmful substances from the body. The effect of congestion is to prevent normal flow and drainage to and from the tissues and organs involved.

The reflex points are used both for diagnosis and treatment: diagnostically, their presence indicates that an organ is congested, while treating the point concerned is believed to relieve this congestion. The anterior reflexes, on the front of the body, are easily located. Many of them lie between the ribs near the breastbone; some lie very close to acupuncture points. The posterior reflexes, at the back of the body, are found along the spine, midway between the spinous processes and tranverse processes (the joints of the vertebrae). In recent problems the reflexes will be very sore or tender; with longer-standing problems they will feel like tiny, stringy swellings under the probing fingerpads of the osteopath.

The osteopath treats them by making small circular movements with the pad of the middle or index finger. He first works on all the anterior reflexes, usually taking no longer than two minutes on each, and then works on the corresponding posterior reflexes. In addition, it is quite often possible to teach the patient or their partner to work on the reflexes between visits; this can help to relieve pain and discomfort, and often speeds up recovery.

CASE HISTORY

A woman of thirty, who was a personal friend, consulted me complaining of excruciating pain in her right knee which had started very suddenly and inexplicably; she had not strained, twisted or injured it at any time. Her general health was very good, she told me, except for constipation, which she had suffered from intermittently for as long as she could remember. Her doctor could find no reason for it, and had advised her to include more fruit, vegetables and fibre in her diet. This advice had helped to some extent, but she did not follow it very consistently.

She had had the knee pain for a week before consulting me. It was constant, and worse when she was sitting. It was bad enough to affect her work, since it not only broke her concentration but she had to leave her desk periodically and walk about to get temporary relief.

I examined and tested her knee locally but could find nothing wrong, and when I examined her lumbar spine and sacro-iliac areas, these tests also proved negative. By now I was very puzzled, and rather at a loss as to the cause of her pain. As I have said, it is against my principles to give generalized treatments; however, as I wanted to help a friend and was certain that there were no contra-indications, I decided to give her some general soft-tissue manipulation and passive articulatory mobilization, hoping that these would at least alleviate the pain. I asked her to come back in two days for re-assessment.

During those two days I studied her case history carefully, and came up with the thought that there might be some connection between her knee pain and her constipation. This led me to look at the location points of the Chapman reflexes, particularly those associated with the small and large intestines.

When my patient returned I was not surprised to learn that there had been no change in her pain after the general treatment I had given her. I immediately started to check for anterior reflex contractions at the appropriate points. Sure enough, when I found them they were tender to the touch. My patient was a little bemused when I started to treat the reflexes on the anterior ribs and along either side of her spine for pain in her knee! I worked on each one for up to two minutes until the tenderness eased.

Next morning I received a telephone call: my patient was delighted to tell me that the knee pain had completely gone. I gave some further treatment to the same points, which proved to be very effective in relieving her constipation. Her knee pain has never recurred, and her constipation has remained much improved through a combination of correct diet and periodic visits to have the reflexes checked and, when necessary, treated.

Pumping and Drainage Techniques

These are techniques within the regime of soft-tissue manipulation which the osteopath uses for specific purposes. Their object is to help the flow of bodily fluids, and improve their drainage.

A popular and commonly used technique for this purpose is a manoeuvre called the 'thoracic pump' technique, which is used mainly in respiratory infections and disorders, and for swelling and engorgement of general bodily tissues. It helps to improve the lymphatic and venous drainage from the chest, abdomen, head and neck areas and possibly the extremities. Its chief effect is to clear a congested chest and relieve any cough. A secondary effect is to produce a gentle motion in the rib cage, helping the respiratory muscles to relax; this enables the ribs to expand more fully, so that the patient can breathe more deeply.

To perform this technique the osteopath stands at the head of the couch with the patient lying face upwards. He places the palms of his hands on either side of the patient's rib cage and then performs a rhythmic, gentle pressure in a pumping action for a few minutes.

Passive Motion (Articulatory) Techniques

Once he has completed his soft-tissue manipulation, the osteopath will normally follow with a form of mobilizing treatment known as articulatory or passive motion technique. To my knowledge these particular techniques are unique to osteo- pathy and are not used in any other form of manipulative medi- cine, including chiropractic.

The method involves moving the restricted joint areas through their maximum range of movements, at the same time applying localized pressure in the direction of the joint restriction. For the patient this treatment is generally relaxing, pleasant and relatively painless.

The principles of this form of passive motion technique can be applied to nearly any joint in the body in need of attention. For example, someone who has recently sprained an ankle may arrive suffering excruciating pain, with the joint inflamed and swollen. In this situation, the osteopath can go to work immediately and apply the technique to the injured part. The osteopath will have the patient lying on his back, and will gently hold the affected foot in both hands, raising the leg up so that the sole of the foot is in contact with his chest. He will then gently and rhythmically work the foot and ankle in small circular and stretching movements never going beyond the patient's pain tolerance. The effect in this instance will be to reduce the swelling by improving the flow of bodily fluids such as the lymphatic and venous circulations; this in turn will help to reduce the pain caused by irritation to the nerve endings. Furthermore, the gentle stretching movement will prevent the formation of adhesions – a very common occurrence after this kind of injury, which, without adequate and correct treatment, will lead to a stiff and possibly chronically painful ankle.

Passive motion techniques can also be applied in conditions where manipulative techniques (described in the next section) are contra-indicated. For example, they are so gentle that they can be applied with confidence to elderly patients whose bones may not be as strong and whose muscles and tissues not as supple as they once were. It is also beneficial in degenerative joint conditions such as arthritis. In my own practice, I have been able to use them to good effect with arthritic knees, for example, relieving pain, improving the mobility and circulation of the joints and toning the associated muscles.

These techniques are extremely useful in both acute and chronic conditions. In acute cases, patients may not be able to tolerate other forms of manipulation; but by employing soft-tissue massage followed by these gentle passive motion techniques the osteopath can prepare the ground for more forceful manipulation, if required, at a later date. On many occasions the restriction is released while the osteopath is putting the affected joint through its motions. This release can be sensed by both patient and practitioner: the joint moves more freely and the muscular tissue around it is more relaxed.

Articulatory treatment can also be very beneficial in chronic conditions, where there may be a lot of stiffness and restriction due to changes in the tissues surrounding the joint. When a lesioned area is left untreated over a long period of time, chemical changes take place leading to adhesions and fibrotic changes, that is, producing thickened, ropy, nodular tissue. The articulatory approach can be extremely useful in helping to stretch and break these down.

Specific Manipulative Techniques to Correct Osteopathic Lesions

As we have seen, the osteopathic lesion consists of a joint whose mobility is in some way restricted. Since the inception of osteopathy, many manipulative techniques have been devised to release these restrictions. Most have been developed from theories about the cause of this loss of joint mobility. Early theories regarded it as a jamming or locking of the joint linkages; the more recent opinion among osteopaths, however, is that the restricted motion is due to muscle spasm or strain. Muscle spasm is therefore seen as the primary disorder in joint dysfunction.

My own view is that either theory can be correct, depending on the circumstances. I believe that when there is a direct trauma

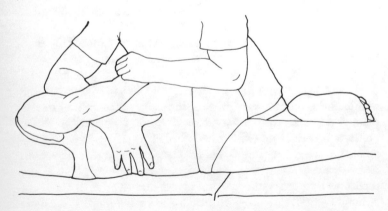

Figure 14. Specific manipulation to liberate tension and restriction in the lower spine.

to the joint – a sudden force or blow that has taken the muscles by surprise – the joint can be forced into a locked position, which will be followed by muscle spasm. The second theory comes into operation when the muscular system is perhaps already fatigued or strained through emotional stress, overwork or bad posture, when a bending or twisting movement can start up a muscle spasm. Here the muscle spasm is primary, and has the effect of splinting the joint, preventing it from moving freely. This is the kind of condition often experienced as something like – 'I just bent down to tie up my shoe lace and my back went!'

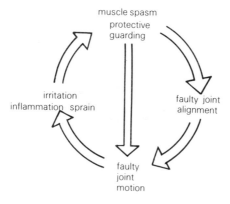

Figure 15. The relationship between a lesion and muscle spasm.

Muscle spasm is caused by the excitatory stimulation of the sensory nerve endings (proprioceptors) within the muscles. The sensory nerves are responsible for relaying messages to the central nervous system (the spinal cord and brain), giving information about muscle activity and tension at the muscle tendon. When muscles are injured the sensory nerves become stimulated and send an increased number of messages into the spinal cord, exciting the relative segment of the cord to send outgoing messages back to the muscle involved, which will increase or maintain the muscle spasm. This, as you can see, creates a vicious cycle. The muscle spasm will cause faulty joint alignment, which in turn will cause faulty mobility of the joint, which in turn will create further irritation, inflammation and possible sprain, maintaining or possibly causing a possible further increase in the muscle spasm.

Manipulative techniques are applied by two methods, direct and indirect.

Direct Methods are familiar to many people for the 'cracks' and 'pops' they produce. It is important to realize that indiscriminate cracking and popping of a joint in itself achieves absolutely nothing. These audible adjustments are only necessary and beneficial when they actually restore normal motion to a restricted area.

While on the subject, you may like to know what causes these noises. Many people believe that they are caused by 'a bone going back into place', but this is not the case. The sound is made by the separation of the joint surfaces causing the vacuum seal of the joint to be released.

Direct manipulation is performed by using high-speed thrusts (referred to by osteopaths as high-velocity thrusts) on the involved joints. They require the body to be positioned beforehand so that the osteopath's manipulative forces can be localized to the specific joint to be treated. To treat the lumbar spine, for example, a classical osteopathic direct method requires the patient to lie on one side. The osteopath will then slowly bend the patient's knees with one hand, until, with the other hand, he feels tension accumulating at the location of the faulty joint. He will then lay the patient's uppermost leg on the couch with the foot tucked behind the opposite knee. He next rotates the upper part of the patient's body backwards, again feeling tension accumulating in the tissues just above the joint. This procedure, which is referred to as 'locking the spine' or 'taking up the slack' has to be performed with the utmost precision: the osteopath must direct his adjustment at exactly the right spot of the lesioned joint. Once he has achieved this, the osteopath will hold the upper body stationary, and gently rock the pelvic region, all the while monitoring the spinal tissues with his fingers to feel for the correct direction in which to perform his thrust on the pelvis.

This thrust is then performed very quickly, and normally a 'pop' will be heard and felt by both patient and osteopath as separation and gapping occurs in the joint. With skilful timing and precision, the muscles attached to the compressed joint will stretch, allowing it to return to a neutral position.

During this manipulative move, the more relaxed the patient is, the more easily the osteopath can achieve the desired result. You don't need to be a contortionist to get into this position, and although it may be temporarily uncomfortable it can usually be applied to the stiffest of spines without undue strain. When it is successful, patients normally report that their pain has eased and they feel a sense of improved mobility.

Direct manipulative methods are frequently used on lesioned joints of the extremities. Controlled thrusts are used to release restrictions in the shoulders, elbow joints and even the small joints of the carpal bones in the wrist and tarsal bones in the feet. Osteopaths are often confronted by patients complaining of a pain in the foot; this is frequently caused by a locked strain of one or more of these small bones, with associated muscle tension. Sometimes the osteopath uses his thumbs to contact the involved bone and thrusts with precision in a simple, con-trolled thrust, using a small, whip-like action which can restore normal joint function and alignment, reducing muscle tension and pain.

Whether the primary cause of the lesion is muscle spasm or a locking of the joints, the thrust-type technique serves to release both. It can be extremely effective, bringing quick and sometimes dramatic results.

Indirect Methods. Over the years some very gentle methods have been developed, which are classified as 'indirect'; they are also well known in osteopathic circles as 'functional techniques'. (They improve the function of the surrounding soft tissues, to improve the mobility of the joint.)

When employing these procedures the osteopath feels for activity in the lesioned tissues by passively moving the affected part and feeling how it reacts. A normal movement gives a sensation of ease and freedom, but when a lesion is present there is a sensation of binding: that is, the soft tissues feel tense to the touch, and the joint does not move freely compared with those above and below it. The osteopath finds the position of ease, at which it moves most comfortably; the effect is to relax the muscles and reduce the excessive discharge of messages the nerves are sending to the central nervous system. This brings about what is called a more 'neutral state' in the affected muscle, in which the muscle is able to function more normally.

This manipulative procedure actually takes the lesioned tissues slowly and gently through the movements which caused the lesion in the first place. It is becoming very popular among osteopaths as it is not only extremely accurate but also non-traumatic – that is, it employs no force and is therefore more comfortable to receive.

Although these techniques do not produce clicks and cracks, it is believed that releasing muscular spasm in this way can also relieve joint restriction and compression. Sickly children and the elderly can be treated with confidence using this approach, since it cannot possibly harm them. I myself have found it extremely useful in very acute conditions, such as acute torticollis, severe spasm of the muscles of the neck, or the acute back, where there is severe spasm of the muscles of the lumbar region.

In this last case, as a rule the patient can hardly move, let alone put on his shoes and socks, and if you ask him to touch his toes so that you can examine him he'll think you're joking! This is where functional diagnosis and techniques come into their own. The osteopath can quietly sit the patient down; with one hand he will move the affected area within its normal range of movement, while feeling and 'listening' to the tissues with the other hand. From this position he will follow through with the treatment, holding the patient in the most pain-free position, until the reactive and painful tissues are quietened and relaxed. It is specific, it is gentle, and what is most important, it brings relief of pain and restores normal tone and function.

Muscle Energy Techniques

These belong to another group of specific manipulative techniques, and are now widely used in osteopathy. They use the patient's own muscle energy to achieve the desired manipulative result. The restricted joint is placed at the limit of the restriction, and the patient is asked to push against counter-force employed by the osteopath in a specific manner. This is repeated several times, and at each repetition the osteopath gauges whether there has been an increase in mobility. This method can be used both on recent and long-standing joint injuries, and is relatively painless.

These techniques have their particular uses and in some cases advantages over more conventional methods. In my own practice, I nearly always correct dysfunctions of the rib cage and specific rib lesions using this approach; indeed, for this area of the body, I prefer it to some of the more conventional thrusting methods.

Respiratory Assistance

While manipulating, the osteopath may ask the patient to assist him by taking a deep breath in, and then making his thrust or applying pressure as the patient breathes out. This serves two purposes. Firstly, it helps the patient to relax. Secondly, osteopaths have noted that during the in-and-out breath, small amounts of movement can be felt between the vertebrae. They can make use of these movements, in combination with the pressures or thrusts, to help them bring about correction with a minimum of force.

Cranial Osteopathy

This is a very interesting technique currently used by many osteopaths, which influences the movement of the cerebrospinal fluid around the brain and through the spinal cord. As it differs considerably from the techniques described in this chapter, and has a wide number of applications, I have given it a chapter on its own (see Chapter 12).

Other Osteopathic Tools

Most osteopaths today find it is worth taking the time and trouble to learn all the different techniques, together with the theories behind them. Once he has become skilled in their use, the practitioner has a wide armamentarium from which to choose, and can select the appropriate techniques for the needs of any particular patient. Some doctors are reluctant to recommend patients to have osteopathic treatment because they have the idea that the treatment will be too forceful. But on many occasions people can be helped by the use of the very gentle techniques I have described.

Osteopathy is certainly not a cure-all system of complementary medicine. Although there are many conditions that can be eliminated, there are many others that cannot be cured completely. Some patients find that they are much better after three or four treatments; others take longer to achieve the same result. Yet others, perhaps because their condition involves more than a musculoskeletal strain, or who have some irreversible degenerative joint changes, may need periodic treatment to maintain the improvements that can be achieved.

Some osteopaths combine their manual skills with other therapeutic modalities, chiefly electrical treatments such as interferential therapy, ultra-sonic therapy, diapulse and diathermy. These are basically used for pain relief, reducing muscular tension, increasing blood flow and stimulating the healing mechanisms of the body. Other osteopaths use heat, in the form of hot towels or infra-red lamps, to help relax the patient and increase blood flow, or cold-water towels or ice-packs to reduce swelling and inflammation.

TREATING THE WHOLE PERSON:

POSTURE, NUTRITION AND STRESS

It should be clear by now that the osteopath takes a holistic viewpoint, recognizing that people function on at least three basic levels: the physical, chemical and emotional. To be truly holistic in his approach, the osteopath must consider not only his patients' physical structure, but also their emotional and chemical aspects, and his treatment should be aimed at restoring and maintaining balance and harmony between all three. An imbalance in any one of the three can not only create a state of ill-health, but can and will also influence the other two. Back and joint problems don't always arise from accidents or injury; the patient's posture, diet, lifestyle and level of emotional stress can all contribute to an imbalance in the musculoskeletal system – and also to ultimate recovery. So, in making a diagnosis the osteopath will want to know not only what is wrong with his patient, but also the original cause of their presenting symptoms. These are also areas in which patients can contribute to their own recovery.

The Role of Posture

Given the importance of the spine, it will be obvious that maintaining a good posture is fundamental to good health. Conversely, faulty posture can lead to a number of ills. It can cause headaches, fatigue, neck tension and back-pain by creating muscular weakness and tension; it can also be responsible for breathing difficulties, malfunction of the internal organs, and strain and dropping of the abdominal muscles and organs, which can lead to conditions like constipation, prolapsed uterus, varicose veins and other problems.

I mentioned earlier in Chapter 3 the importance of the

fascia, or connective tissue, and particular bands of fascia have an important function in correct posture. The most common areas of fascial strain associated with postural imbalance are in the gluteal buttock areas, the outside of the thighs known as the tensor fascia lata, the lumbodorsal fascia which is three-quarters of the way down the back, and the cervical fascia or neck region. Abnormal tensions in these areas can produce pain, usually a burning sensation due to pressure on the sensory nerve endings contained within the fascial bands. These stresses and strains on the fascial bands can be palpated, and are given important consideration in the osteopath's overall examination.

Good and Bad Posture

What is the ideal posture? When a person stands upright, the onlooker should be able to imagine a straight line running down the side of the body, passing through the ear, through the shoulder, through the centre of the upper arm, through the hip and the centre of the upper thigh, and through the knee, finishing just in front of the ankle bone. From behind, a similar straight line should run through the centre of the back of the head, along the mid-line of the spine, through the crease of the buttocks down to midway between the feet. And from the front, the line should pass through the centre of the forehead, mouth and nose, down through the mid-line of the breastbone, through the navel, ending midway between the feet.

Given today's lifestyle and environment, it is understandable that many people are not in the habit of sitting or standing correctly. Contributory factors include unsuitable shoes, and badly designed furniture and car seats. High-heeled shoes, for instance, tilt and rotate the pelvis forward, conditioning the muscles to hold the pelvis at an incorrect angle. There may also be congenital factors: a common anatomical defect is the 'short leg', which can be caused by the bone or bones of one leg being shorter than the other from birth, or as the result of a bad fracture.

But much of the time we are victims of our own bad habits, such as slouching, or standing on one leg and hitching the pelvis up on one side. If a 'short leg' has been caused by muscular contractions brought about by spinal lesions and misalignment of the pelvis through injury, standing in this unbalanced way can make it worse. A bad habit many women adopt is to hitch up one hip to carry a baby or toddler; this also creates muscular imbalance in the pelvis and spine which eventually leads to pain in the lower back and possibly further up the spine. (So if you have to carry a baby, stand evenly on both feet, holding the baby in front of you, with one hand under its bottom and the other on its back.)

Many people sit badly, with their spine slumped, often for long periods of time, which stretches and strains the ligaments and muscles of the lumbar region. This not only weakens the lower back, but also can lead to problems elsewhere, by causing distortion and strain of the shoulders and neck. It is true that badly designed furniture encourages bad posture; but we can still make a point of sitting squarely on our buttocks, maintaining the pelvis in a vertical position, thus keeping a natural lumbar curve.

The Effects of Postural Distortions

Let us look at some of the postural distortions that osteopaths commonly encounter, and their effects on the body as a whole.

Starting with the side view, many people push the chin up and forward, which accentuates the normal cervical curve and places tension in the neck. As a result the neck becomes shorter and the spinal nerves and vessels passing through the intervertebral foramina may become congested and pinched. This can cause pain in the region of the shoulder blades, referring down the arms, with paraesthesia (pins and needles) in the hands.

Together with this increased cervical curvature, we normally find an exaggerated curvature in the thoracic spine, giving the appearance of round shoulders (kyphosis) and a hunched back, and narrowing the chest. This can create pressure on the diaphragm and rib cage, causing breathing difficulties as well as impairing the circulation of blood and lymph. Muscular tension and pain may well be felt in the middle of the spine between the shoulder blades; anyone suffering from this aching-type pain will know how fatiguing it is.

Still looking at the side view, the osteopath frequently finds that the pelvis is tilted forward, increasing the normal lumbar

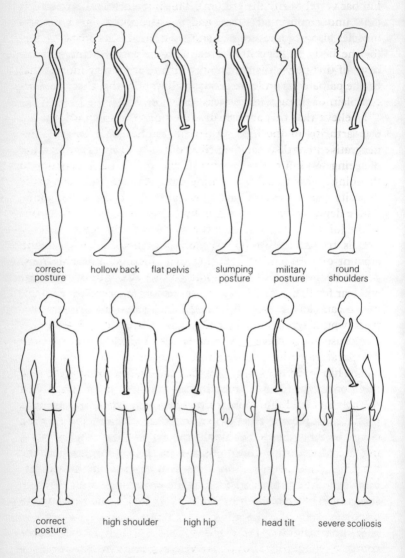

correct posture   hollow back   flat pelvis   slumping posture   military posture   round shoulders

correct posture   high shoulder   high hip   head tilt   severe scoliosis

Figure 16. Correct and incorrect posture.

curve and creating a hollow back (lumbar lordosis); this imposes a particular strain on the lumbosacral joint (formed by the fifth lumbar vertebra and the sacrum). This puts the disc between this joint under continual stress, and the associated ligaments and muscles also become strained and tense, as it is a constant effort for the body to keep itself erect. I come across some extreme cases of this pelvic distortion, in which nearly every muscle that can be palpated is under tension; small wonder that these patients complain of tiring with the least exertion.

I believe that this abnormally tilted pelvis also contributes to osteoarthritis of the hips. Osteoarthritis has been called a degenerative joint disease; it is believed to arise from a combination of ageing and injury or excessive strain, which causes irritation to the joints. This leads to a wearing down of bone cartilage, while deposits of new bone tissue appear at the margins of the joints. These deposits, known as osteophytes or spurs, reduce the space of the joint cavity, restricting the mobility of the joint.

It is true that everybody's joints are subjected to a certain amount of wear and tear during their lifetime. Probably most people over forty will show some normal evidence of this wear and tear for their age. However, some show an excessive amount, which can cause pain and limited joint movement. Most osteopaths would agree that faulty alignment within the joint, such as that caused by incorrect posture, can lead to early and excessive degeneration within the weight-bearing joints.

The hip joints are formed by the heads of the femurs (the long thigh bones) which fit into cavities each side of the pelvis. When the pelvis is held unnaturally tilted forward, excessive tension is produced in the muscles both surrounding the joint and running down the thigh bones. Eventually the mobility of the hip joints is impaired, resulting in stiffness and an irregular motion of the femur head inside the cavity. The loss of elasticity in this weight-bearing joint and its surrounding tissues makes it much more susceptible to the stresses of wear and tear, leading to osteoarthritis.

While considering the pelvis, we have to include the all-too-common condition known as 'visceroptosis', which means a dropping or displacement of the abdominal organs. Although it can have various causes, the most common is a loss of tone in the pelvic and abdominal muscles. This leads to a protruding and dropped abdomen, which in turn affects the inner organs, including the stomach, colon, small intestine, liver, spleen and kidneys. Symptoms can include indigestion with dragging pain and a bloating fullness, constipation, back pain, vertigo and headaches.

The osteopath may not be able to cure this condition fully, but he can definitely help over a period of time by giving gentle abdominal manipulations, which will improve not only the tone of the abdominal and pelvic muscles, but also the circulation and function of the congested and dilated organs. The osteopath will also give attention to the patient's faulty posture by manipulating the pelvis, spine and extremities, while manipulation of the appropriate spinal centres will stimulate blood flow, improving the circulation and function of the organs.

The osteopath will also recommend daily exercises to help improve the tone of the weak muscles. In addition, he will advise the patient to restrict his diet and avoid distending the abdominal contents further.

Very often the osteopath will prescribe exercises individually, particularly for overweight patients who may also have high blood pressure. However, you may like to practise the following exercises on your own to improve your posture and prevent future problems.

Exercises to Improve the Posture

Before giving any corrective exercises, the osteopath will show you how to correct your posture by standing tall, with your head up and chin in, chest expanded and up, but not held stiffly or puffed out. Your shoulders should be down with the arms hanging loosely, abdomen tucked in and the buttocks slightly tensed. In this posture, the imaginary lines described on page 88 will be correctly positioned, and your body will be under the least strain.

If you are checking your posture on your own, use a full-length mirror. You may be shocked at your usual way of standing! I know many of my patients are appalled when I point out their postural irregularities! Faults to look out for which indicate poor posture and also muscular imbalances and faulty joint alignment (i.e. osteopathic lesions) that are worth noting:

- Look to see if your ears are level. If not this could indicate a tilting of the head due to imbalances in the neck muscles, and the possible presence of spinal lesions in this region.
- Look at the level of your shoulders: you may find one higher than the other.
- Check that your pelvic bones are level: you may notice that one hip sways out more to one side than the other.

If you do find postural imbalances, please take my advice and spend some time improving your posture in front of the mirror. Since this isn't always easy to do on one's own, it may be a good idea to visit an osteopath, who would be pleased to help you to correct any imbalance. Please remember one thing: it takes time and effort to change a poor posture to a correct one. So work on it, but be patient.

The following exercises are very useful for releasing the tired tension aches that result from poor posture. Don't do them, however, if you have a definite back pain: *do* seek a consultation with an osteopath.

Do them once or twice a day, up to three times each.

EXERCISE 1

From the standing position described above, take a deep breath in, at the same time stretching the whole spine upwards, raising the shoulders at the same time and keeping the feet flat on the floor. Hold this position for a count of five, then breathe out as you relax back to the basic standing position. This helps to stretch the whole spine.

EXERCISE 2

From the basic standing position, raise the shoulders as in Exercise 1. Take in a deep breath and bend the trunk from the hips to the horizontal position, still maintaining the raised position of the shoulders and keeping the spine straight. Return immediately to the upright position, still with the shoulders raised and a straight spine, relax back to the basic position and breathe out.

normal standing posture

exercise 1

exercise 2

exercise 3 (a)

(b)

(c)

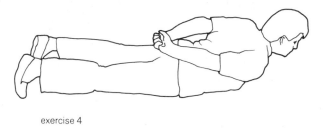

exercise 4

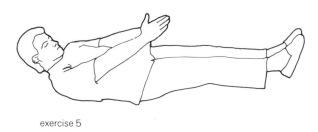

exercise 5

Figure 17. Postural exercises.

EXERCISE 3
From the basic position, bend the trunk until it is horizontal, this time with the arms by the side, elbows bent and hands held together against the chest. Breathe in and at the same time raise the arms upwards, level with the head. Breathing out, slowly move your arms in a circle, outwards and backwards, finishing with them back by your sides. This exercise strengthens and tones the spinal muscles and helps to prevent round shoulders.

EXERCISE 4
Lie face down on the floor with the spine straight, clasping your hands behind your back with the elbows bent. Keeping the pelvis flat on the floor, raise the upper part of the body, at the same time extending the hands and arms backwards. This exercise is very helpful for counteracting round shoulders.

EXERCISE 5
Lie on your back on the floor, with your legs, body and head in a

straight line and your arms by your sides. Breathing in, lift the feet approximately six inches off the floor, simultaneously raising the head to look at the feet. Holding this position, raise your arms, keeping them straight, and clap your hands together in front of your body. Breathe out as you relax back on the floor.

This exercise is very good for toning up the abdominal muscles and can be repeated as many times as is comfortable, taking care not to over-strain. If performed daily, the number of repetitions can be increased gradually as muscle tone improves.

Walking, and the Importance of the Feet

One of the best forms of exercise you can take is walking – provided you do it correctly. Unfortunately, many people these days have lost the ability to perform this very fundamental act, and their feet and posture suffer as a result. I often despair when I watch people walking with stiff, shuffling steps, with their arms held tensely at their sides or, worse still, their hands in their pockets. Walking correctly can give you a much healthier, more mobile body, as well as being more enjoyable.

This makes the feet very important, designed as they are by nature to support the body and to absorb the shocks and vibrations caused during walking, running and jumping. Mechanical problems in this area can reflect problems throughout the rest of the body.

The mechanism of the foot is dependent on the normal function and alignment of the bones which make up the arches. Each foot contains twenty-six bones arranged into two arches, the 'transverse arch', and the 'longitudinal arch', which is divided into two sections, the medial and lateral arches. The arches act as leverages to spring the body forward as we walk.

The first essential requirement is to avoid walking with the feet turned out, as so many people do, but to turn the feet and toes very slightly inwards. This is the natural position: just watch a baby taking its first steps! Try a little experiment, and see what happens when you stand with your feet turned slightly in. You will find that the foot automatically arches, because this position brings into use the muscles of the foot and lower leg, which maintain a normal arch. Standing like this is the first basic correction for flat feet.

The next important factor in correct walking is to avoid shuffling! One practitioner has described correct walking as 'like going upstairs, but on the flat'. You should let the heel strike the ground first; the weight then passes to the ball of the foot, which springs the body up and forwards as the foot leaves the ground. In conjunction with this, you should take reasonably long strides, letting the hip swing forward with the leg rotating the pelvis: this keeps the foot in its correct position as the leg moves forward. This action not only allows longer strides but also exercises the pelvic joints and lower spine, especially the fifth lumbar vertebra, which articulates with the pelvis.

For perfect coordination, balance and rhythm, let the arms swing loosely and naturally, the left arm swinging forward at the same time as the right foot. This also exercises the thoracic spine and keeps it mobile.

Walking correctly can not only prevent troubles from developing, but can help quite severe problems to improve, as we shall see when discussing osteoarthritis (see page 165–7).

The Chemical Overload

One of the principles of osteopathy is that our bodies contain self-regulatory mechanisms to help maintain their own health. These mechanisms protect us by providing immunity against internal and external influences, such as viruses and pollutants. They help to regulate the function of our vital organs; they initiate a repair process for damaged and injured tissue, and help the body cope with irreversible conditions such as arthritis. Without these self-regulatory mechanisms, no form of therapy could take effect. Osteopathy helps the body to heal itself.

I have already touched on the importance of diet in relation to overweight and its effects on the spine, internal organs and so on. But there is another aspect to nutrition, which is its importance to health generally and, very often, its effect on musculoskeletal disorders. Some osteopaths have also trained as naturopaths, and will pay particular attention to diet. However, most osteopaths these days have had considerable training in the role played by nutrition and will inquire about their patients' diets, particularly if they suspect that a disorder or pain may be connected with a nutritional problem. Over recent years, most osteopaths in clinical practice have noticed an increase in the number of patients presenting with symptoms of chemical overload. (A list of these symptoms is given below.)

This increase is almost certainly the result of the increased popularity and availability of convenience foods – 'junk' foods – which not only have minimal nutritional value, but also contain chemicals that are harmful to the body. I personally do not believe it will harm most people to eat the occasional hamburger or fried meal; the body has an eliminative system designed to rid it of unwanted chemicals. But the too frequent and over-heavy consumption of such foods amounts to an abuse of this system, leading to body pollution and ill-health.

Unhealthy nutrition is not the only cause of chemical overload; another all-too-common cause is the over-use of medical drugs, or, worse still, a combination of pills and poor food. In order to cope with this chemical pollution, the internal organ system has to work extra hard, and may end up functioning poorly as a result.

If an osteopath fails to recognize the signs of a chemically overloaded body and simply applies structural and mechanical treatment, he is liable to achieve only poor results. For successful treatment, he needs to be able to recognize the signs of stressed and malfunctioning organs. Many of these will become obvious during the initial taking of the case history and observation of the patient. For example, any or a combination of the following symptoms will indicate a chemical overload:

Frequent dry mouth
Metallic taste in the mouth, especially noticeable on awakening
Dark circles under the eyes
Skin rashes with itching
Red blotches suddenly appearing on the skin
Muscular soreness all over the body
Pains down the arms, particularly the right arm
Pain between the shoulder blades
Pain at the base of the skull with headaches

Stiff necks or the condition known as torticollis (wry-neck) where
   no strain or injury has occurred
Severe low-back pain which has come on suddenly for no appar-
   ent reason
Leg pains throughout the entire length of the legs
Lethargy and fatigue
Irregular bowel motions
Bad breath with strong body odour

Thus, if the patient mentions during the initial consultation that
he suffers periodically from severe low-back pain for no obvious
reason, or complains of a stiff neck unrelated to a specific injury
or even a minor strain, the osteopath is alerted to the possibility
of a chemical overload.

   The osteopath can also palpate and recognize this organic reflex
disturbance through the contracted muscular tissue adjacent to
the involved spinal area. As I have explained, organs under stress
can create stress within the spinal column, through what is known
as the viscerosomatic reflex. The malfunctioning organ initiates
further stress within the nervous system by setting up a relay of
adverse nerve impulses to the segment of the spinal cord to which
the organ relates, giving rise to muscular contractions in that
area. These muscular contractions differ from the traumatic
spinal lesion in that they usually span over three or four vertebral
joints rather than being localized at one vertebral joint. Very
often, the area concerned is the segment relating to the liver and
gall-bladder, organs which are particularly susceptible to chemical overload.

   In such cases, the osteopath can aid elimination by 'pumping'
the liver and gall-bladder areas, using a gentle form of manipulation which the recipient generally finds relaxing and relieving.
He can also give specific osteopathic treatment to the spinal areas
relating to the distressed organs, in order to damp down the
nerve impulses and assist the nervous system, using the technique
known as inhibition. This consists of applying pressure over the
spinal segment concerned, varying in intensity from light to heavy
according to the age and size of the patient and the severity of the
symptoms. It is a useful form of treatment whenever there is any

excessive activity and overload in the body's structure and function.

However, in dealing with conditions like this, no amount of manual treatment alone will solve the patient's problems. He or she will also need to be counselled and given advice about their dietary habits. Sometimes the osteopath will recommend adopting a strict regime, avoiding certain foods and chemicals. This is often the hardest part of the treatment, for he has to convince the patient that their stiff neck or low-back pain is caused by organic stress resulting from a poor diet. This is especially hard when the foods involved are those the patient likes and enjoys the most – such as chocolate, sweets, sugar, highly seasoned foods, cream, butter and fried foods. Drink is also important: excessive amounts of coffee, tea, soft drinks like lemonade, and alcoholic drinks can all lead to an overload of the system. The osteopath can only guide and advise his patients to eliminate these items from their diet: the rest is up to them.

Normally, certain foods need only be totally eliminated for a short time, to give the body a rest and help its systems to re-balance. After recovery it is often possible to reintroduce them – but in moderation, to avoid a recurrence of the problem. During the acute stage, the osteopath will recommend drinking plenty of spring water (rather than tap-water, which tends to be full of chemicals); this helps the liver, gall-bladder and kidneys by flushing unwanted chemicals out of the body.

When my patients follow this advice to the letter, many of their ailments are eliminated, and it is quite common for them to tell me, 'I haven't felt as well as this for years!' To help them *stay* well, it is usually necessary for the osteopath to educate and encourage them into adopting the more natural and healthy diet as a lifetime's habit, not just a temporary fad.

Of course, the osteopath must never lose sight of the possible presence of a more serious pathological condition which requires medical treatment. If a patient does not respond to dietary change within a very short time, or if other symptoms indicate it, the practitioner will refer them for an in-depth medical examination. Sometimes it may be necessary for gall-bladder or kidney stones to be removed, and I have found on several occasions that these surgical operations have eliminated a patient's back-pain.

Below are some general guidelines for healthy eating which I recommend to my patients, and follow myself.

(a) Try to eat as many fresh foods as you can; in particular, increase your intake of raw salads and vegetables.

(b) When cooking, do not use aluminium utensils. Boiling removes much of the nutritional value from foods, so steam vegetables or use other waterless methods of cooking.

(c) Cut down on (preferably eliminate) white flour and sugar products. For preference use wholemeal flour, and for sweetening, raw cane sugar and/or honey.

(d) Cut down on all meats, especially red meats which contain the most fat and are acid-forming. Substitute with more fish and white meats.

(e) Cut down on all dairy products – eggs, cheese, milk and butter. These are highly acid-forming, as well as mucus-forming.

(f) Keep your salt intake to the very minimum. Excessive amounts can, in the course of time, lead to hardening of the arteries, high blood pressure and fluid retention!

(g) As far as possible avoid tinned and processed foods, which usually contain a high concentration of chemicals and pre-servatives.

(h) Drink plenty of fresh spring water, pure fruit or vegetable juices, and low-tannin and decaffeinated tea and coffee. Do not pump your children full of 'pop' drinks, with their high sugar and chemical content.

(i) Get into the habit of eating a piece of fresh fruit rather than cake or chocolate.

(j) Never rush meals, chew well, and eat in a relaxed atmo-sphere.

(k) Don't overeat, eat at regular intervals and avoid eating near bedtime. Your stomach needs as much rest as you do!

(l) Drink alcohol in moderation only.

(m) About smoking – *don't*!

CASE HISTORY

The 52-year-old manager of a turf accounts' business consulted me for pain between his shoulder blades, in his neck, and under his skull, spreading over his head to the frontal region above the eyes. He had been suffering from these for three years; he did not feel that they were created by stress, though they caused him stress and tension since the pain was making him irritable and depressed. Nor did he feel that they were particularly related to any physical strain or injury. He told me that he would simply wake up with these pains, which could last for three or four days and then go away for a day or two, only to return for no apparent reason.

He had already had a good deal of treatment before coming to see me. First, he had had some X-rays taken, which showed some arthritis and wear and tear in his lower cervical spine. He had been prescribed a course of physiotherapy, which did not help. Next he had consulted an osteopath who treated him with a combination of osteopathy and acupuncture, also to no avail. In desperation, he consulted a friend, who recommended him to see me.

I, too, nearly fell into the trap of treating him from a purely mechanical and structural viewpoint. When I examined him I found tension and restriction in the mid-thoracic spine and the lower and upper cervical spine. I also found that his blood pressure was rather higher than average for a man of his age. He told me that his appetite was good, although he suffered a little discomfort at times with indigestion. I believed that treating the mechanical problems I found in his spine could be the answer to most of his symptoms, even possibly his high blood pressure; it is not unknown for blood pressure to reduce once restrictions have been released in the spine.

After four treatments of osteopathic adjustments of the spine, all the lesions had been eliminated except for those in the mid-thoracic region. These would be much relieved immediately after treatment, but they always returned and were present when I palpated him on the next visit. Although the lesions in the neck had been eliminated, the man was still not better, and there was no change in his blood pressure readings.

Now, the troublesome area on the thoracic spine was segmentally related to the gall-bladder and liver, which made me begin to think in terms of possible organic overload in these organs. Without explaining what I had in mind, I asked my patient to make a list of all the food and drink he consumed during the following week and to bring it on his next visit.

When I read the list I was horrified to see the amount of junk food and coffee he was getting through. I immediately advised him to eliminate all these from his diet, explaining to him that his body was probably suffering from chemical overload. He accepted this and followed my advice.

Within two weeks he began at last to feel some improvement. After three weeks, he was symptom-free, and his blood pressure had dropped to within normal limits. When I last saw him he had not been troubled with his spinal pain or headaches for six months, and was even managing to eat the odd bar of chocolate or fried meal and drink the occasional cup of coffee with no ill-effects – but he assured me that for his own benefit he now took these foods only in moderation.

I should make it clear that chemical overload is not responsible for every pain or ailment that people may suffer from. But, when it is correctly identified and treated, dealing with it may well help some people who have been classified as hopeless cases after consulting several therapists without success.

The Effects of Stress on the Musculoskeletal System

Osteopaths see many patients who are suffering not only from physical tension, but also from emotional stress. Of course, pain from musculoskeletal injuries can cause emotional stress, usually manifesting itself as irritability or depression. I have lost count of the number of times I have remarked to new patients that they seem depressed, for them to retort: 'Wouldn't you be depressed if you had my pain?'

Severe or long-standing pain certainly causes stress, through loss of sleep, fear of what may be wrong, fear that the pain will go on for ever, and worry that time lost from work will lead to employment and financial difficulties. In these cases, successful osteopathic treatment not only relieves the pain but also the accompanying stress, and the patient returns to normal.

However, as osteopaths recognize, emotional stress can reflect through to the musculoskeletal system. In fact, it can create a myriad symptoms, ranging from changed (usually raised) blood pressure, loss of or excessive appetite, irritability, depression, sleeplessness, headaches, tiredness, lack of energy, gastric discomfort leading to ulcers, pain and tightness of neck, shoulder and back muscles, colitis (irritable bowel) and hyperventilation (over-breathing). This list could be even longer, but it gives some idea of how stress can and does affect us.

We are all different, and one person's stress may not take the same form as another's. One person may suffer neck and shoulder tension pains, while another will suffer abdominal tension with indigestion pains. The question arises here as to why stress affects different areas of the body in different people. Osteopaths believe that one possible answer is the osteopathic spinal lesion. As we have seen, the spinal lesion has an excitatory effect on the central nervous system, and in particular on the spinal cord segment that is related to the lesion via the nerve fibres. This area is, or can become, vulnerable to any other stimulus such as prolonged emotional stress. This in turn can affect the areas of the body such as the muscles, tendons and organs related to the disturbed spinal segment, causing pain and disturbed function within these structures. Thus the lesion exacerbates the condition, and must be taken into consideration regardless of other contributory factors.

Our bodies possess built-in emotional mechanisms which create specific feelings like fear, apprehension, worry, aggression, envy, hatred, sadness – and of course happiness and joy. These are natural reactions to our everyday encounters and, when the nervous system is working in a positive and balanced way, they can help us to protect ourselves by responding appropriately to threatening situations. However, in many instances, prolonged and continuous stimuli cause these reactions, either singly or more often in combination, to get out of balance. The central nervous system which should regulate them becomes fatigued, and then exhausted, resulting in the condition we have come to recognize as stress.

In these cases the osteopath may need to play a psycho-therapeutic role as well as a physical one. This happens very naturally, usually while the osteopath is giving some form of manipulative treatment, so that psychotherapy is an integral part of the treatment. An osteopath who is tactful, relaxed and a good listener can build a relationship of mutual confidence with his patient, which is of great importance if the patient's emotional stress is to be helped. Very often all that is needed is a 'listening ear'. Some osteopaths have a natural ability to give advice and to reflect their own positive attitudes, stimulating their patients to take positive steps towards dealing with their emotional states. Sometimes osteopaths will refer patients to qualified counsellors or psychotherapists, and they will always refer patients to special-ists if they are suffering from deeper mental illnesses which are clearly beyond the osteopath's scope.

When my patients are suffering from tension arising from stress, I prescribe breathing exercises* which help to reduce both physical and emotional tension. I practise them myself, so I can personally vouch for their efficacy. The best time to do them is in bed at night as they will help you fall asleep. They can also be done at other times of the day, if you wish; for the best results, I recommend you to try to stick to the same time each day.

STAGE 1: DIAPHRAGMATIC AND ABDOMINAL BREATHING

1. Lie flat on your back with your hands lightly resting on your stomach. As you take a deep, slow, comfortable breath in-wards, feel your stomach rise; at the same time try to fill out the small of your back with air, by slightly pushing the back downwards.
2. Exhale gently and slowly, allowing your stomach to fall.
   Do this for fifteen minutes each night for a month.

STAGE 2: FIVE-STEP SEGMENTAL BREATHING

1. Lie flat on your back and practise breathing as above, until you are breathing freely and easily. Now, starting with your toes, imagine that you feel a warmth, or that someone is

* Modified from a book I bought many years ago, *Sleeping Through Space* by Alexander Cannon, 1939, published by the Walcott Publishing Co., Woodthorpe, Nottingham.

touching you, or visualize a bright light in that area. Next, imagine this warmth, light or touch travelling up to each knee as you breathe in, and back to the toes as you breathe out. Do this for about three minutes.

2. Now imagine the warmth, light or touch travelling up from your knees to your groin as you breathe in, and from the groin back to the knees as you breathe out. Do this for about three minutes.

3. Now imagine the warmth, light or touch travelling from your groin to your solar plexus as you breathe in, and from the solar plexus back to the groin as you breathe out. Continue for about three minutes.

4. Imagine the warmth, light or touch travelling upwards from the solar plexus over your chest and up to your larynx (the hollow at the base of the throat at the top of the breastbone) as you breathe in, and back from your larynx to your solar plexus as you breathe out. Continue for about three minutes.

5. Imagine the warmth travelling from your larynx up the sides of your neck over your ears to about two inches above the top of the head as you breathe in, and back down to the larynx as you breathe out. Continue this until you fall asleep.

CHAPTER SEVEN

TREATING THE LOWER BACK

(I) THE 'SLIPPED DISC'

The Causes of Low-back Pain

The so-called 'slipped disc' or disc lesion is probably the best-known and one of the most frequent causes of low-back pain. However, it is far from being the only one, and low-back pain is a very widespread problem. In July 1985 it was reported by the Office of Health Economics (an independent research body founded in 1982 and funded by the drugs industry) that back-pain costs the nation:

- £1 billion in industrial output, through absence from work
- Over £156 million on National Health Service treatment
- £195 million paid in sickness benefits to workers taking time off
- A total of thirty-three million working days of certified incapacity

As these figures show, back-pain is approaching epidemic proportions.

Low-back pain, incidentally, is often described as 'lumbago', but this commonly used word is not a specific diagnosis and can cover a multitude of disorders. Most osteopaths do not use the term, preferring to be more specific in their explanations to patients.

One of the major causes of back-ache is undoubtedly injury to the musculoskeletal system, caused by accidents such as falls, and by unnatural twisting movements (at work or during sports) which jar and strain the muscles and spinal column. People who have been in car accidents also frequently suffer from back-pain afterwards.

Another cause is strain, which can be brought about by repeated incorrect lifting, or by lifting beyond one's capabilities.

Incorrect sitting or standing, at home or at work, can also weaken the spine by putting it under constant strain; and the man or woman who is continually stooping over the sink, workbench or car engine may well end up with back problems. Osteopaths or consultants often tell such patients that the way they are sitting, standing, lying or lifting is contributing to cause their back-pain, but the working environment often makes it extremely difficult, and at times impossible, to do these things in an ideal way; this is probably one reason why back-pain is so prevalent.

Even as I sit here writing, I am putting my lower lumbar spine under some strain – but when I have finished I will counteract it by going through the postural exercises described in the last chapter. Being aware of your posture and correcting it whenever you can will help to minimize this kind of strain and guard against an increase in back-pain. (Further guidelines on caring for your spine are given at the end of Chapter Eight.)

A high percentage of women report that their back-pain problems started after having their first child. I believe that osteopathic examination and treatment should be considered as soon as a woman decides to start a family. If osteopathic lesions and dysfunctions are found in the spine and pelvic region these can and should be treated prior to conceiving, to avoid or minimize back-pain during pregnancy. To me, taking this precaution makes absolute sense, since any mechanical problem with the spine or pelvis, no matter how minor, will be aggravated by the increased pressure and weight created by pregnancy.

Overweight is another condition that often contributes to back problems. Carrying an excess load makes the spinal column more vulnerable to injury and strain, and an injury sustained years before can be exacerbated by a sudden weight gain. The osteopath will encourage such patients to lose weight through a sensible diet; together with osteopathic adjustments this often relieves their pain. Reducing weight has other rewards, too, since it helps to remove strain on the cardiovascular system (the heart and circulatory systems), thus enhancing and promoting better health all round.

All these considerations should be taken into account, both by the osteopath and the patient. It is a waste of time for the osteopath to give precise adjustments to the spine if the patient leaves his practice rooms and immediately afterwards abuses his back by indulging in the very activity which has contributed to his problems in the first place! I am constantly surprised by patients with back-pain who are not aware that they should take things easy for the time being. Many are under the impression that being under treatment is enough, and that they can carry on as usual without having a role to play in their recovery programme. Good osteopaths should take the time to discuss these points with their patients, and to advise them about rest and preventative care after recovery.

Allied to low-back pain is sciatica, another common problem with a number of possible causes. Sciatica is the name given to severe pain running along the course of the sciatic nerve. This is the largest nerve in the body, supplying directly or through its branches the hamstring muscles, the muscles at and below the knee joint, and those of the foot. It also supplies large areas of the skin of the leg and foot. One cause of sciatica is osteoarthritis of the lower lumbar spinal joints creating irritation and pressure on the sciatic nerve; sciatica can also be associated with other conditions such as diabetes mellitus (a faulty secretion of insulin), gout, and some vitamin deficiencies. The most frequent causes, however, are osteopathic lesions of the lower lumbar spine and sacrum, or the condition popularly known as the 'slipped disc'.

What Is the Slipped Disc?

Contained within the spinal column are twenty-three discs. They are found between the bodies of each vertebra, from the sacrum at the bottom of the spine to the axis, the bone at the top. Each disc has an outer wall, made up of a tough, fibrous, cartilage-like material, known as the *annulus fibrosus*. Contained within this is a gel-like substance which is soft and pulpy-looking, similar to toothpaste; this is called the *nucleus pulposus*. The role of the discs is to act as shock absorbers between the vertebrae when they are under forces of compression. They also help the spinal column to move, since they broaden or flatten between the vertebral bodies as the spine is bent one way or another.

To refer to a 'slipped disc' is really misleading. It implies that a disc has actually slipped out of its place between two vertebrae, but this does not – and cannot – actually happen. However, the term is often used by doctors, osteopaths and other manipulators since it is an easy one for patients to grasp, without going into too much technical explanation.

A disc can be weakened or injured, for example, by sudden compression during lifting, or when a person falls heavily on their feet or buttocks, or by the more repetitive strains of lifting, bending, twisting and gravitational stresses. As a result it can become herniated or ruptured. Some people consider that there is no difference between herniation and rupture, but to many – including osteopaths – there is a difference, and this difference is important in the management of the disc syndrome.

When a disc is herniated the outer wall, the *annulus fibrosus*, bulges out and may impinge on and compress the spinal nerve root, which can cause excruciating pain. (Sometimes the disc can bulge without resting on a nerve or irritating pain-sensitive structures, in which case very little pain will be felt.) In many cases, osteopathy can reduce the disc bulge and relieve the pressure on the nerve.

A ruptured disc is a condition in which the gel-like substance in the centre protrudes through the outer wall, which has been weakened by degeneration and tearing. In this case, surgery is normally indicated.

Sometimes a patient may have been told that he has a degenerated or 'thinned' disc. This can be the natural result of ageing, or of wear and tear from constant strain or repeated minor injuries. It can cause back-pain, usually fairly mild; even so, it can give rise to a nagging-type ache, which can be distressing. The thinned disc is usually responsive to osteopathic manipulation, although the patient may need to attend regularly every month or six weeks to maintain the relief and improvement.

It is extremely difficult to make an accurate diagnosis of the disc syndrome. While X-rays are helpful to osteopaths in ruling out bone disease and detecting degenerative bone pathology, they are rarely helpful in establishing whether a disc is herniated or ruptured. The discs themselves cannot be seen on X-rays; only the distances between the vertebrae can be seen and measured.

An X-ray may sometimes show a decrease in the space between two vertebrae, but it cannot show whether the wall of that disc is bulging and impinging on a nerve.

A more helpful method of investigation is myelography: this consists of taking X-rays after the injection of a dye, which can be seen running down the spinal cord; a disc lesion or any other space-occupying lesion will then show up as an interruption in its flow. However, even this is not conclusive evidence as to whether the outer disc wall is intact and whether the disc bulge may be reducible by manipulation. Even a positive finding may not prove that the disc is causing a patient's pain since, as mentioned above, some disc bulges produce no painful symptoms. And another drawback of myelography is that it can produce unpleasant short-term side-effects in the form of vomiting and headaches.

So you can see that, whatever diagnostic method is used, it is difficult to differentiate between a herniated, bulging but intact disc wall, and a ruptured disc whose outer fibres are torn and split with the gel-like fluid protruding through. Although the osteopath can be guided by clinical signs and symptoms, it is only by actually trying out treatment that he can tell whether he will be able to reduce the disc bulge.

Ruptured discs are less common than herniated discs. In 1932 a Dr Schmorl reported dissection studies of ten thousand cadavers and found that fifteen per cent of these showed disc lesions; however, only two showed traumatically ruptured discs. It usually takes a very severe accident or injury to rupture a normal disc, and this rarely occurs as a result of a minor trauma.

On most occasions disc herniation takes place following a direct injury, usually of a compression nature, causing a downward pressure on the disc. For instance, one case I treated, with a suspected disc herniation, was a man who had missed a step down while carrying a bag of cement on his shoulders, which caused a jolt through his spine into a lower lumbar disc. Another cause of herniation is a period of continued minor injury or strain, which can potentially weaken and injure the disc, eventually leading to herniation.

The most common area for disc lesions is undoubtedly the

lower back, between the fourth and fifth lumbar vertebrae and the fifth lumbar and the sacrum. The erect stance adopted by mankind places a good deal of pressure and weight-load on the spinal discs, especially when postural faults develop such as the forward tilting pelvis with its associated increase in lumbar lordosis (a hollow back), exaggerating the curvature in the small of the back. This situation can create a shearing strain leading to compression of the lumbosacral disc (between the fifth lumbar vertebra and sacrum), making it more prone to injury and eventual herniation.

Patients who consult osteopaths with a suspected disc lesion are normally in a great deal of pain. This is usually felt in the lower back and buttock muscles accompanied by pain referring down the leg along the sciatic nerve. Coughing or sneezing may make it worse; so can attempts to bend, either forwards or backwards. The sufferer may observe that their body contour is twisted, due to the pull of the muscles in spasm, with one hip swaying outwards. In severe cases the opposite shoulder can be seen to sway away from the affected hip, giving the patient a crab-like walk. This may look funny, but there is nothing amusing about this extremely painful condition.

The pain is actually experienced in the tissues surrounding the disc, such as the ligaments, nerve root and the articular cartilage which lines the vertebral joint, tissues which are pain sensitive and can be affected by a herniated disc. It is not felt within the disc itself, since it is generally accepted that this has no nerve supply. This is why many disc injuries go unnoticed at the time they occur; pain is not felt until the next morning, when the disc has swollen and is pressing on the pain-sensitive structures.

Osteopathic treatment does not consist of putting the disc back into position as is sometimes erroneously believed. When manipulation is successful, this is because the osteopath reduces the muscular and postural tensions and releases pressure from the disc; this reduces the disc bulge so that it no longer presses on the pain-sensitive tissues.

CASE HISTORY (I)

As a newly fledged osteopath one of my first encounters with a disc condition was the case of a man of thirty-seven; he weighed sixteen and a half stone, and walked into my consulting-room in the crab-like manner described above. After the routine consultation and examination I laid him face-down on the couch, the position which seemed most comfortable for him, and busily went to work to sedate the contraction and extreme tension in his back muscles. When I had spent some minutes working in this manner I asked him to get up and turn on to his side. To my horror, the man could not move, and it took me about ten minutes of struggle to get him up! When he was finally on his feet he was clearly no better: in fact his back muscles appeared to be in further spasm and his postural distortion worse.

I quickly thought the problem out and concluded that laying him on his stomach had caused further pressure on the disc by dragging on the tissues. I asked him to lie down again, this time on his side, and repeated the soft-tissue treatment and manipulative techniques until I felt a reduction in the muscle spasm and some improvement in mobility. This time, when I asked him to stand he was able to get up with comparative ease, he stood straighter than before and had less pain.

I certainly learned a lesson from this experience: never to lie acute disc cases on their stomachs. In fact, I have found that all acute back pain responds much more quickly if I work with the patients either lying on their sides or on their backs, and I advise nearly all my patients with low-back pain to avoid sleeping on their stomachs.

I am happy to report that after four treatments this particular man's back was much better. Once he was better I strongly urged him to lose weight to help maintain the improvement – and still do, when I see him from time to time, without making much impression, I'm afraid!

CASE HISTORY (2)

A woman of thirty-four hobbled into my consulting-room, complaining of severe pain in her right buttock, thigh and calf. The pain was so intense that it made her limp; any attempt to walk normally sent shooting pains up and down her leg. In addition, she had symptoms of paraesthesia (pins and needles) of the right foot and anaesthesia (loss of feeling) in the right calf.

I spent some time on the consultation. She told me that all these symptoms had started eight months before, with a back-pain which was now only a dull ache, and nothing compared with her current leg pain. Her problem had started after a work-out in a gymnasium, using light weights; she was new to this form of exercise, and had probably entered into it over-enthusiastically. No definite injury had occurred during the work-out, and she was in no pain at all when she left the gym, but the next morning she awoke with low-back pain: her problems had begun.

Before consulting me she had received treatment from her local hospital, consisting of pain-relieving epidural injections and physiotherapy. X-rays had also been taken in which, she was informed, nothing abnormal had been detected. She was then prescribed a corset and told that an appointment would be made for her in the near future to see an orthopaedic surgeon. As you can imagine, by this time she was feeling very sorry for herself; the pain was making her tearful, depressed and at times irritable.

When I examined her I found that bending forward caused a dull ache in her low back and increased the pain in her leg; she had to bend the affected leg, as keeping it straight was intolerable. When I tested her ankle reflex by tapping the tendon at the back of the heel, her foot did not jerk as it should, which showed that there was some pressure on or blockage to the nerves supplying particular muscles in the affected leg. Lifting her leg while she was supine (a procedure called the 'straight leg raise') exacerbated her pain. And when I examined her lower back I found that the muscles on both sides, and especially on the right of the spine, were contracted, feeling hard and tense to the touch. All these signs and symptoms indicated that the sciatic nerve was being irritated, probably due to a disc lesion.

I began treatment with spinal soft-tissue massage, with the aim of releasing the tight lower back muscles; I then used manipulative techniques to improve the structure and function of the areas of the spine and pelvis above and below the disc lesion, releasing pressure away from the suspect disc. After the first treatment the patient reported that she felt a little easier and more relaxed. However, since her visit to me, her local hospital had contacted her, asking her to return for further treatment three times a week. I encouraged her to take up this offer as I could not at that time guarantee a cure, and I knew that her financial resources were limited.

Three months passed and then one morning she telephoned me in a very distressed state. I gave her an appointment, and when she arrived she gave me an update of the treatment she had undergone over the last three months. This included an epidural injection, a plaster corset, and traction, which she found very uncomfortable and did not help her condition. Finally, after a myelogram, she had been told that there was a disc problem between the fifth lumbar and the sacrum, and that she would be scheduled for a surgical operation.

After re-examining her, I decided to continue as before, treating the muscle contraction and restricted areas of the spine with gentle, controlled manipulative techniques designed to re-lease the pressure and help reduce the disc bulge. I am pleased to say that after six treatments her symptoms were much better, and she was able to lead a normal life again without the ex-cruciating sciatic pain.

By this time the hospital had arranged for her to consult the orthopaedic surgeon who was prepared to operate. When she saw him she told him she had been visiting an osteopath, and after examining her, the surgeon advised her to carry on with the osteopathic treatment.

After that she attended periodically and when I finally dis-charged her she had no symptoms except for a slight loss of feeling in her big toe. That was three and a half years ago; I contacted her recently, and she told me that she is living a normal life, without pain.

CASE HISTORY (3)

A woman of fifty-one, a professional radiographer, consulted me for pain in the lower back, referring down the back of the left thigh and calf muscle. She had previously received two treat-ments from an osteopath, which had not seemed to help, and had then consulted an orthopaedic surgeon who diagnosed her con-dition as a 'disc lesion'. He prescribed fourteen days' bed rest followed by fourteen days on traction. None of this relieved her pain, so he scheduled her for a myelogram with a view to possibly performing a spinal operation. The patient turned this down as she had heard that there might be side-effects to myelography; instead she decided to give osteopathy another chance and came to see me.

She described the pain in her leg as being rather like toothache. It was aggravated by walking, standing, coughing and sneezing. The only thing that eased it was lying flat on her back. I had no reason to doubt the surgeon's diagnosis, but on examining her I found multiple osteopathic dysfunctions of her sacro-iliac joint and lesions as far up as her lower thoracic spine. I discovered that her primary problem was a twisted pelvic bone, technically called a pelvic torsion lesion (this condition is described in Chapter Eight). I thought that if I could correct this it would release her considerable muscle spasm and relieve the pressure on the lumbosacral disc, the suspected site of the disc lesion, thus allowing the herniation to reduce.

I began treatment, and after six visits she showed definite signs of improvement and was able to cut down on her painkillers. After the ninth treatment she had improved a great deal and her condition was only aggravated when she had to walk any distance. After the twelfth treatment she was very much better, free of pain and able to walk without discomfort.

After a few periodic visits to make sure all was well, I discharged her. Three years have passed since then, and when I recently contacted her I was delighted to hear that she has had no further problems, apart from the occasional very temporary twinge.

Self-care for Disc Problems

In suspected disc cases the osteopath will advise his patients on what to do and what to avoid. Taking this advice can sometimes be as important to recovery as the treatment itself.

I recommend periods of rest during the acute stage, when the disc problem is recent and very painful. But I also advise patients to have periods of activity to maintain the tone of the spinal muscles, such as walking round the house for a short while and then returning to bed rest, or gently lifting the knees up to the abdomen, one at a time or together. You can also lift one bent leg and gently rotate it in small circles, then lower and repeat with the other leg. Sometimes both legs can be raised, keeping the knees bent, and gently rocked in small movements from side to side. While performing these movements, on no account must the head or upper trunk be raised at the same time as the knees, as this creates too much flexion stress in the lower back.

To reduce inflammation and to improve the circulation in the tissues surrounding the disc, osteopaths may recommend applying an ice-cold compress, made by putting ice cubes in a plastic bag and laying them on a cold, wet towel over and across the involved area. This can be applied for fifteen minutes at least three times a day.

I find that many disc lesions respond well to this all-round approach, combining inhibitory soft-tissue treatment, precise spinal adjustments and self-care. Patients who show no signs of improvement after a reasonable period of time are referred back to their doctor to seek the advice of an orthopaedic surgeon. As mentioned above, some cases do require an operation, but it is generally well-worth trying osteopathic treatment first.

Further guidelines for the care of your back are included at the end of the next chapter. If you have a disc problem, incidentally, do not do the exercises for posture described in Chapter Six as this is a very different problem.

CHAPTER EIGHT

TREATING THE LOWER BACK

(2) OTHER LOW-BACK PROBLEMS

So far we have looked at low-back pain caused by disc problems. Discs, however, are by no means the only cause of low-back pain. Among the many other conditions that can cause aching and disabling lower backs are specific muscle spasms, pelvic lesions and injuries to the small joints of the lumbar spine. Most of these can cause pain similar to that of the disc lesion, and simulate a disc problem. It is therefore very important that they are diagnosed correctly, so that the right treatment can be given and pain relieved as quickly as possible. Over the years osteopaths have become very skilled at diagnosing and correcting the problems I shall be describing here. Indeed, some of these conditions are only specifically recognized by osteopaths or similarly qualified manipulators.

Psoas Spasm

This is a common problem which brings patients into osteopathic consulting rooms. It involves spasm of a group of muscles within the abdomen, the largest and most important of which is the psoas major, which attaches to the front of the lumbar vertebrae and descends to attach to the inner thigh bone. These muscles help the body to bend, and also play a part in walking. When in spasm they can cause the pelvis to shift to one side, pulling the torso forwards and to one side of the contraction, and giving the body a twisted, distorted appearance.

Psoas spasm is very often caused by flexion stresses in the lumbar spine, such as assuming a bent-over position for a long time, or sitting slumped in a soft armchair for long periods. Other common causes are exercise – especially over-straining while doing sit-up abdominal exercises, injury, and cold draughts. Predisposing conditions include a straightening of the normal lumbar curve through faulty posture, and abnormal bone conditions causing instability and weakening of the lower back. It has also been noted that excessive emotional stress can lead to psoas spasm.

When the muscles go into spasm, the pain is usually quite severe at the base of the spine, the area known as the lumbo-sacral area. Pain is also commonly felt in the buttock and over the sacro-iliac joint, which connects the sacrum to the pelvis. It is accentuated by any attempt to bend backwards and, as described above, the sufferer tends to hold himself forward in a bent position. Although the pain is at its worst at the base of the lumbar spine, the osteopath usually finds fixations of the upper lumbar spine, and this is the primary area for his treatment.

Before attempting to release and mobilize the spinal fixation, the osteopath will use reflex techniques to reduce the muscle spasm, followed by spinal manipulation to help reduce it further. During the acute stage the osteopath will apply his treatment very gently – an over-vigorous manipulation will be too painful for the patient, and will not help the condition.

A word of warning: people often apply heat to their backs as soon as they feel discomfort, but this is definitely the wrong treatment for the psoas spasm mechanism. There is already an inflammatory congestion in the area; heat causes vaso-dilation, an increase in the expansion of the blood vessels, and will therefore only make the problem worse by causing further congestion. Electric heating-pads are particularly bad for this condition, and will change a mild spasm into a severe and painful one.

Exercises can play an important part in the treatment and prevention of further spasms of this muscle group. They are best performed once the acute stage has been managed. The osteopath will advise patients when the time is right, and will prescribe specific exercises suited to each individual. He will encourage patients to maintain these long after treatment is ended, for a really bad, acute psoas spasm is a very painful condition that is best avoided, and there is a danger of it recurring if the patient relapses into bad postural habits.

I believe that if a psoas contraction is allowed to go untreated and becomes chronic, it can eventually lead to disc problems. This muscle group is unique in that its fibres are the only ones to insert into a specific ligament attached to the disc, known as the annular ligament. There are other, less obvious conditions to which a psoas involvement can contribute. They include respiratory disorders, since the psoas muscles also have a close connection with the diaphragm, the chief muscle involved in breathing. Some digestive disturbances have been known to improve once the psoas has been treated, including hiatus hernia; correcting the psoas can greatly assist in the tolerance of this condition.

Pelvic Lesions

Another problem area commonly associated with low-back pain is one or other of the two pelvic bones which connect with the sacrum to form what are known as the sacro-iliac joints. These joints are vulnerable to both injury and strain. The osteopath often discovers a positional problem here, i.e. faulty positioning of one pelvic bone in relation to the other, which causes pain and problems of mobility within the sacro-iliac joints.

It was once thought that sacro-iliac joints could not move, but for many years osteopaths have maintained that microscopic movements do take place; this has since been proven by a number of medical authorities. Osteopaths get very good and often dramatic results when performing precise and careful manipulation on a sacro-iliac joint, and over the years they have perfected a number of techniques to achieve correct function and structural relationship.

A common problem in this area is a *pelvic torsion lesion*, or twisted pelvis. Here, one pelvic bone has twisted either backwards or forwards as compared with the opposite pelvic bone. A pelvic torsion lesion can cause incapacitating low-back pain, and aching-type pain running down the thigh of the leg on the involved side, as well as pain in the groin. Because of these symptoms it may be wrongly diagnosed by the patient's doctor as a disc lesion. The existence of this type of lesion can also have far-reaching effects on the whole spinal column, as various spinal curvatures may form in the body's attempt to compensate for the twisted pelvis.

The most common type of pelvic torsion lesion is the backward type. This is normally caused by trauma, usually by a force coming upwards from below: for example, missing a kerbstone and stepping heavily down on one foot can cause a powerful jolt which travels up from the foot through the thigh into the sacro-iliac area, causing the pelvic bone to change position, twisting backwards on the bone of the sacrum. As I have mentioned, pain is experienced on the side of the lesion in the sacro-iliac area, sometimes in the groin and sometimes referring down the thigh. In the acute stage it can be incapacitating; the sufferer will be unable to put on his shoes and socks, and will make any movement with extreme caution.

If the condition is allowed to become chronic the pain will be less severe, becoming more of a dull nagging ache, which can be exacerbated by standing still for a period of time as well as by walking, and it will definitely be aggravated by running. An interesting symptom that can also arise from this problem is an aching type of pain felt on the inside of the knee. When the osteopath's local examination of the knee proves negative, with no ligament or cartilage problem or degenerative arthritis, he will suspect the presence of a sacro-iliac problem.

When a specific diagnosis has been made, corrective treatment will be given to restore correct alignment of the pelvic bone, which will also restore normal mobility within the sacro-iliac joint. This not only reduces pain and allows the ligaments and soft tissues to heal, but produces better function and structural relationship throughout the whole body. Since the pelvis acts like a structural platform, any lesion in the pelvic field is liable to have not only local effects, but also far-reaching effects on other structures and functions in the body.

It may take some time to achieve full correction of this lesion, but the pain can usually be reduced in only a few treatments.

CASE HISTORY (I)

A rugby player of thirty-five was complaining of pain in his right lower back and buttock area, referring into the right groin and down the back of the right thigh. He had been suffering with this for three months before coming to see me. The pain had started after a rugby injury when he was hit in mid-air by an opposing player while he was jumping up for the ball, and landed heavily on one foot. He felt an immediate sharp, stabbing pain in the right sacro-iliac low-back area, and needed the attention of the club physiotherapist. He tried to go on playing, but after a further ten or fifteen minutes had to leave the field.

Next morning he found it extremely difficult to get out of bed and had to get his wife to put on his shoes and socks for him. He went to see his doctor the same day, and was prescribed pain-killing tablets and a week's bed-rest. As a result he did feel better and resumed his daily activities, but he was aware of a continual dull ache persisting in his lower back. Eventually this became worse and began to refer to the groin and thigh, and at this point he was prompted to consult an osteopath.

On examination I found a pelvic torsion lesion with one pelvic bone twisted backwards on the right. This was causing some shortening of his right leg, which was probably also due to the muscle contraction in his back and leg. Correction by a controlled and precise thrust to the pelvic bone restored the joint to its correct position and levelled the leg lengths. He was in much less pain after the first treatment and almost symptom-free after the third. Four weeks later, on his fourth visit, he reported that he was completely free of pain, and on examination I found the pelvic bones were in correct relationship to one another.

CASE HISTORY (2)

A young girl of twelve was brought in by her mother suffering from an aching pain at the medial side of her left knee joint. She had had it for six or seven weeks, and neither she nor her mother could think of any accident or injury that might have caused it. The pain was not constant, and was mainly aggravated by walking or running, but it would last for a few hours after these activities.

I examined the knee very carefully and could find no signs of injury, strain or disease to the local muscles, ligaments or joints. I did begin to wonder if the girl was faking the pain, perhaps to gain attention, but I decided to give her the benefit of the doubt and proceeded to examine her sacro-iliac area. Here I found a definite restriction in mobility on the left side, and the left iliac bone was held in a restricted, backward position. The child was not aware of any pain here until I palpated the ligaments of the joint, which she described as 'very tender'. I used a non-thrusting type of correction to reduce the lesion.

On her second visit she reported that she was much better, and her mother told me that when they got home from the initial consultation her daughter had remembered that while she was skipping in the school playground a few days before the knee trouble had started, she had landed awkwardly and felt a sharp pain in her lower back. The following morning, however, she had seemed quite all right; she and her mother had forgotten all about it and had had no reason to connect it with the knee pain. After another three treatments at weekly intervals, she was completely recovered, and her pelvis was restored to its normal positional relationship.

As these two stories show, if you have a heavy fall, even if there is no apparent damage, it is worth having an immediate osteo-pathic check-up – it could prevent a lot of problems developing!

CASE HISTORY (3)
This is an example of a lesion of the anterior, or forward twisting type. A man of forty-six came to see me complaining of pain in his left buttock, which had started four and a half months before. He described the pain as static: it was getting no worse, but, unfortunately for him, it was not getting any better. He could recall no injury or accident relating to the onset, and was not aware of what had actually started the pain. He also remarked that over the last few months he had been suffering more con-sistently than usual from digestive upsets and constipation.

On examination, I found that he had a pelvic dysfunction; one pelvic bone was twisted forward out of its normal alignment, with associated tenderness and tension of the hamstring muscle on the same side. This structural problem can sometimes be associated with bowel and digestive disorders and simultaneously with the Chapman's reflexes described in Chapter Five.

Manipulative treatment successfully restored the malaligned pelvic bone. I also applied massage-type treatment to the relevant Chapman's reflexes, which not only relieved the pain in the buttock, but also brought about a return of normal bowel movement and eliminated the digestive disturbances.

Not all forward twists of the pelvic bone need Chapman's reflex treatment but some osteopaths have found a close connection between these soft-tissue reflexes and pelvic torsion, especially when there is no history of injury or trauma. As yet we have no explanation as to why this should be so.

Another pelvic lesion that osteopaths come across quite commonly is the result of one pelvic bone being shifted in its position directly upwards upon the sacrum (the triangular bone at the base of the spine). This is caused by falling or landing heavily on one side of the buttock, when the force of the impact pushes one pelvic bone upwards without any twist. There is often an increase in this type of injury in winter weather, when people slip on the snow and ice. It can produce low-back pain as well as pain in the buttock and thigh.

Because of the nature of the injury that produces this type of pelvic lesion, it is often necessary to have X-rays taken in order to rule out a fracture before treatment is given. If there is no fracture, treatment can be started immediately. This is relatively simple and normally painless for the patient. The osteopath grasps the patient's ankle with both hands and turns it inwards so as to lock and protect the hip joint; then he gives the leg a quick tug, which pulls the pelvic bone back downwards to its normal position.

In my experience this problem usually requires no more than one manipulation, but in addition the osteopath will check and if necessary give further treatment to the spinal joints in the lumbar region, which may also have become lesioned through the impact of the fall.

Sacral Lesions

The sacrum, the triangular bone at the base of the spine, could be called the foundation of the vertebral column. It has been said that an abnormal tilt of this bone can cause widespread tensions throughout the body, while correction of these lesions has been known to result in the relief of pain higher up in the back, even releasing tensions as high up as the neck. Osteopaths often find that lesions elsewhere in the spine will not stay corrected until the level of the sacral base plane has been restored.

One common sacral lesion is known by osteopaths as a *sacral torsion lesion*. This is believed to be caused through strain or force being transmitted through the spinal column down to the sacrum: for example, by a golfing swing, where the trunk and spinal column are twisted and the force of the movement is centred into the sacrum, causing the sacrum to twist out of its normal alignment between the two pelvic bones. I have found such lesions many times among golfing enthusiasts!

The movement of the sacrum, as I have mentioned, is very small; but it can be detected and palpated by osteopathic diagnosis. This is carried out by testing the mobility of the sacrum and feeling for positional changes. The condition of the spine, particularly the lumbar area, can also aid in the diagnosis of sacral lesions, since it will be held in a distinct pattern of stress by the neuromuscular contractions involved. This postural distortion can look very like the bodily leaning and pelvic side-shift involved with disc lesion, and very often patients have come to me with 'disc lesion' diagnosed by another practitioner which has turned out to be a sacral torsion lesion.

The sacral torsion lesion can be responsible for low-back pain; the malposition of the bone imposes a strain upon its ligamentous attachments, and can cause a mechanical strain at the lower lumbar joints. In my experience, the distribution of pain can either be central, spreading across the lower back, or to one side, in the sacro-iliac and buttock area.

It can also lead to problems elsewhere in the body. Many osteopaths, myself included, believe that if this lesion is not corrected and is allowed to become chronic, a number of further problems may well build up as a result. Firstly, the lesion will create tensions in the muscles which keep us erect, especially the psoas muscles which are so important in maintaining the correct curve in the lumbar spine. Secondly, strain and stress will develop through the ligaments of the sacrum and pelvis. And thirdly, since the sacrum is the base on which the spine sits, if it is not level it can create spinal curvatures which will lead to an uneven distribution of weight and stress through the spinal discs; disc degeneration and lesions can follow.

A senior osteopathic practitioner in America, Dr Harold I. Magoun, has done a great deal of research into the effects of the sacral lesion. In his paper on the subject (1965), he goes so far as to state that if the sacral base is abnormal every tissue of the body is put under strain, resulting not only in mechanical disturbances of the joint, but also in circulatory and lymphatic disturbances. Thus the sacral lesion not only disturbs the mechanical balance of the spine, but can also affect the blood and lymph supply to the foot, ankle, knee and leg; with this impairment of the circulatory systems, varicosities (varicose veins) are common. He also warns that all too often a bodily pain can be mistaken by doctors for a visceral (organic) ailment; for example a pain located under the right shoulder blade with no local findings may be tentatively diagnosed as a liver or gall-bladder disorder. Then, when on careful and thorough investigation no visceral disorder can be found, the doctor may regard the patient as a neurotic who is imagining or inventing his pain. The osteopath, who is aware that mechanical joint disturbances can cause remote pains, can often offer some hope in these cases, where a thorough medical examination has been made with no positive findings, by finding and treating a musculoskeletal dysfunction in the sacral area, quite far from where the pain is felt.

Most sacral lesions can be corrected by osteopathic manipulation. On this particular area many osteopaths prefer to use the gentle, indirect methods rather than more forcible direct manipulation. One reason for this is that the sacro-iliac joint, of which the sacrum is of course a part, only requires to move slightly. Too many thrusting type manipulations could create too much movement, stretching the already strained ligaments; this could weaken the joint, making it vulnerable to even minor strains which would not normally cause problems. So osteopaths are careful not to over-manipulate this joint; although occasionally a thrusting type of manipulation is needed to restore physiological function and position, its use is kept to a minimum.

Lumbar Joint Lesions

Osteopaths have been studying the physiology of the spine for many years and have become experts in how it moves and behaves during our daily activities. This study has enabled them to diagnose and interpret the many strains and injuries that occur within our backs. In the lumbar spine the joints allow the spine to flex, extend and side-bend with only a small amount of rotation. When a twisting movement is made while the lumbar spine is bent or stretched to its near or full capacity, the joints can become susceptible to injury. A common example is when someone bends down with the legs straight to lift something from the floor, and while picking it up twists the body to put the object on a surface. This involves two basic mistakes: one should always bend the knees to lift something from the floor, and rather than twist the body, turn straight on to face the surface you want to place the object on.

Any mechanical problem affecting the joint facets which link the lumbar vertebrae can cause pain and loss of movement in that area. A major cause of disturbance in these joints is trauma, such as injury caused by a sudden, inappropriate movement, especially when a force is introduced into the joint when it is already at the limit of its possible range of movement. Osteopathic treatment can release these tensions and restrictions, restoring normal movement and eliminating or greatly reducing pain.

CASE HISTORY
A market trader aged thirty-two consulted me one Saturday for acute low-back pain. At the market that morning he had picked up a small tarpaulin sheet which he used to cover the framework of his stall, and had thrown it over his shoulder. Immediately he had felt a severe pain in his lower back.

This is a typical way in which such a lumbar joint lesion can occur. You may be able to visualize the movement of the body and spine: the man's lower lumbar spine was bent forward nearly to its full range; then, as he threw the tarpaulin over his shoulder he twisted his lower back, which was already under strain. In addition, the weight of the tarpaulin landing on his shoulder would have created a jarring effect at a specific joint area, compressing the spinal joints and causing pain, together with muscle spasm and congestion of the lymph and blood vessels around the joint.

He was in great pain, which was exacerbated by any movement involving his lower back. When I examined his lumbar spine, I could feel an increase in temperature over the skin between the fourth and fifth lumbar spinal segments, indicating an acute lesion. When I palpated this area, he described it as 'very sore and painful', and testing the mobility of the joint confirmed that there was a mechanical disturbance at the fourth and fifth lumbar facet joint.

I asked the patient to lie on his side, and gave inhibitory soft-tissue manipulation to the muscles that I felt to be in spasm, slowly pulling the muscle mass of the back away from the spine to stretch the contracted tissue and help relax the injured and irritated tissues. As explained in Chapter 5, this soft-tissue treatment can be very soothing and relaxing for a patient in pain, and prepares them for the next stage of treatment – manipulation to release the restricted joint.

My personal approach to an acute lesion like this is to use a very slow and gentle stretching release manipulation. This can be tolerated by the patient and can bring good results, as it helps reduce the congestion around the lesioned joint; very often both the osteopath and patient can feel the tension and restriction release. (I prefer this approach to the sudden high-speed thrust which increases the inflammatory congestion around a recent, acute lesion. The high-speed thrust is more beneficial with longer-standing lesions, when the joints and tissues will have become somewhat restricted.)

I used the slow, gentle approach on the market trader, and we both felt a release at the joint concerned, accompanied by a quiet popping sound as the vacuum seal of the joint separated. When he stood up and moved around he felt considerably easier, and was able to put on his shoes himself. I told him to rest over the weekend, to avoid sitting in armchairs, in order not to stiffen up, and not to bend from the back: if he really needed to pick something up, however light, he should bend his knees to reach for it.

When he arrived for his second appointment on the Monday he was feeling much better, with only a mild aching pain at the base of the spine. After another three treatments he was totally pain-free, and there were no signs of the lumbar lesion.

This is typical of many acute back-pain cases seen by osteopaths: if the damaged back can be treated quickly and efficiently the patient will be able to return to work without too much delay. Generally I have found that osteopathic treatment gets the patient better much more quickly and efficiently than the orthodox medical treatment of bed rest and pain-killers. However, sometimes a combination of all three can prove to be very beneficial in the early stages of back injury. Osteopathic treatment will speed recovery and the patient will therefore need to take fewer drugs and spend much less time in bed.

A useful aid in treating very recent and painful sprained backs is for the osteopath to apply adhesive tape to the area in a specific manner, after giving manipulative treatment. The taping helps to support the lower back muscles, which promotes quicker healing of the tissues. Usually the tape needs only to be left on for three days, after which it can be removed and manipulative treatment continued.

Once the patient's back is back to normal, the osteopath will give extensive advice on how to keep it that way by showing him how to lift, bend, stand and sit correctly. I have included much of this advice at the end of this chapter.

Other Low-Back Problems

Among the other low-back problems for which people consult osteopaths, a common condition is the chronic degenerative spine which may be diagnosed by X-ray as spondylosis or osteoarthritis (which will be discussed more fully in Chapter 10). These patients can and do obtain relief through osteopathic treatment; the results are not as dramatic as those obtained by releasing a purely mechanical joint problem, but a number of patients have been thankful to be able to carry out their daily activities with less pain, and are often able to reduce their drug intake to a minimum.

Unfortunately, there are some low-back problems which may not be manageable by or responsive to osteopathic methods, or which it may even be unwise to treat by osteopathy. The osteopath is trained to recognize such cases and to refer them for appropriate medical treatment. They include bone fractures, malignancy of bone, bone infection such as osteomyelitis, active bone disease such as rheumatoid arthritis, active osteoporosis (bone softening) and disc lesions where the protrusion is large enough to cause pressure on the spinal cord causing serious neurological symptoms.

How to Care for Your Back and Spine

Any practitioner or therapist who deals with back pain is aware of the importance of good posture, and osteopaths are no exception. 'Good posture' has been discussed in Chapter 6, but it involves not just how we stand, but how we sit, walk, lie down, work and play. All too often, we adopt positions and postures that tire the back muscles, straining them and leading to back-pain.

You can help yourself to avoid back-pain by adopting the guidelines listed below: for them to be really effective you should build them into your daily activities so that they become second nature.

- You can prevent trouble by following the postural improvement routine described in Chapter 6 – but don't do these exercises if you have an acute disc or other back problems.
- *To prevent strain during everyday activities*, switch from one task to another before fatigue sets in. For example, if you are a

housewife, avoid spending too much time in one session at the ironing-board or the sink; find another task in between times in which you can use a different posture and muscles. Anyone who has to sit at a desk for long hours should make opportunities to get up and move around, and to exercise the neck and shoulders, especially by drawing the shoulders back. Desk-workers should also do frequent spot-checks to make sure they are sitting correctly.

- *When sitting*, a back's best friend is a hard, straight-backed chair, which helps to keep the neck and back in as straight a line as possible. Rounding the back and sitting on your lower spine puts a strain in the neck and shoulders and can cause what's known as 'dowager's hump'. Sit with both feet flat on the floor, and avoid twisting the spine by crossing your legs.

- *When standing* for long periods, change position frequently, and avoid putting all your weight on one hip or the other. It helps to rest one foot on a footrest, frequently alternating the feet; this relieves a sway-back, a hollow back.

- *Always bend* from the hips and knees, keeping the back relatively straight, and never bend from the waist only. It is worth remembering that the thigh and leg muscles are much more powerful than the back muscles.

- *Lifting and carrying*. Always face the object you wish to lift, and never twist your spine while lifting. (This is a very common cause of back pain.)

- Always keep the object you are lifting or carrying as close to your body as possible.

- Never carry or lift an object or load that you cannot manage with ease, and never lift anything very heavy higher than your waistline.

- Always try to avoid carrying uneven weight-loads, which can distort the spine and cause uneven contractions, straining the spinal muscles.

- When lifting, never hold your breath, but learn to breath deeply and regularly.

- *Avoid making sudden movements* which can take the muscles unawares (for example, jumping up from the chair to answer the phone).

- *When lying down*, try to keep the head, neck and back in as straight a line as possible.
- Avoiding lying on your stomach while in bed.
- It is usually beneficial to have a firm mattress, but before investing in an expensive bed, experiment by putting a board under your mattress.

WHAT TO DO WHEN YOU HAVE ACUTE BACK PAIN

- Always seek professional advice immediately it occurs. It may be detrimental to 'wait a few days and see how it goes'.
- At this time plenty of rest is very important, and it is essential to have a firm mattress.
- While resting, either lie on your back with pillows underneath your knees or on your side with the knees bent. Both these positions help to take the strain off the lower back muscles allowing them to rest.
- Never get straight up from lying on the back into a sitting position; turn on to your side first, and then use your arms to help yourself sit up.
- If total bed rest is ordered, some gentle exercises should be performed to aid recovery to the muscles and promote circulation; they also help to keep the bowels regular. All exercises should be done while lying on the back with the knees bent – never straighten the legs. The exercises should be kept simple; for example, while lying on your back, place the hands round one knee and gently rock the knee towards your chest. This can be followed by gently making small circles with the knee in this knee-to-chest position. Repeat with the other knee. Don't over-do them! If these movements aggravate the pain, they should be abandoned until such time as you can do them without an increase in pain.
- When the back feels strong enough and is capable of supporting the body, get up and move around now and again between rest periods, but don't overdo it.
- Once you are up and around, avoid working in stooped positions, such as bent over a car engine, sink or workbench. Unfortunately, there are times when our work or environment demands adopting these positions. Obviously, if you can get

someone else to make the bed or do the washing up, all the better. If not, make it as easy for your back as you can, for example by kneeling to make the bed, and lowering or raising work surfaces.

WHAT OSTEOPATHS DO WHEN THEY GET LOW-BACK AND SPINAL PAIN

Yes, unfortunately, even though osteopaths know the rules of the game, they too can suffer the distressing symptoms of back-pain. Their work involves a good deal of standing, bending, lifting and twisting; even though they take every possible precaution, it can be quite physically demanding, and an osteopath who is tired is at risk of a strain.

So what does the osteopath do when he finds himself in trouble with a nagging back? Obviously the first step is to seek his own medicine from a colleague. Some time ago a colleague's wife telephoned me in a panic asking if I would come and attend to her husband who was incapacitated and confined to bed. That morning he had bent down to shift the door-mat at his consulting-rooms when he was struck down with severe pain in his lower back. By his own admission he had been overdoing it that week, because he was going on holiday the week after.

When I visited his house I found him confined to bed, and I literally had to lift him on to the portable couch I have, which is specially designed for home visits. I gave gentle soft-tissue and osteopathic treatment to the facet joints and muscles of his lower back, after which he could walk cautiously without help. After this first treatment his wife was able to drive him to my practice, where I gave him three more similar treatments. These saw him at least fit enough to go on holiday! Fortunately for me, he returned the favour when I strained my lower rib cage at a later date.

After that we agreed that we should give each other treatment periodically so that we could both stay in shape and prevent our problems from recurring. We did this for several months, but since we both had busy practices we ran into an increasing time problem. Then, to my delight, I found a solution in the form of a set of exercises which provided a means of manipulating our own

exercise 1

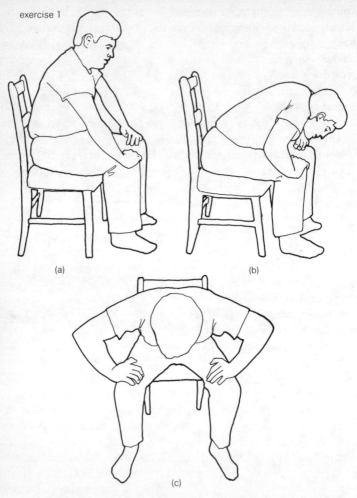

(a)

(b)

(c)

A gentle exercise for the lumbar spine, which can be performed shortly after an episode of acute lower-back pain. Sit on a chair, and place your hands just above your knees, with your fingers pointing in towards themselves. Your arms should be straight (1a). Bend your upper body forward, supporting all your weight on your arms and allowing your elbows to bend, until you reach the point of pain restriction in the lower back (1b). Hold this position for a moment, then, using your arms as levers, bounce up and down gently and rythmically for a few seconds (1c). Return to the starting position. Repeat the exercse five times.

Figure 18. Preventative exercises (after Chester E. Kirk, DO).

spines to keep them supple and fit (Kirk, 1977). By following Kirk's routine daily (it only takes about ten minutes) I find I can keep relatively fit and supple and I don't have to trouble my friend so often, although I still have an osteopathic check-up and treatment once in a while.

These exercises are illustrated left and below. I have also found them useful for my patients, especially when their treatment has ended. If they practise them regularly they can avoid recurrences of their back-pain and return visits to my practice. However, I also advise them to contact me immediately if there is any sign of their pain returning, and to stop the exercises for the time being.

exercise 2

(a)

(b)

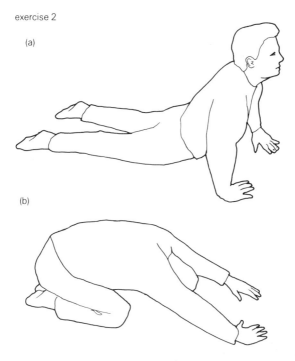

Lie on your stomach, and place your hands, pointing inwards towards each other, under or just ahead of your shoulders. Using your arms as levers, raise the top half of your body so that your back is arched backward (2a). Now arch your back the other way, and roll your body upwards and back until you are sitting on your heels (2b), with your chin tucked in towards your chest. Roll forward again to the starting position. Repeat the exercise five times, moving rhythmically between the two positions.

exercise 3

(a)

(b)

(c)

Lie on your back with your arms outstretched. Draw up your knees until they are at an angle of about 90° to the floor. Cross one leg over the other, and let the weight of the leg gently roll the pelvis and the lower spine over to one side (3a). Once in that position, rock to and fro in a rythmic motion for a few seconds. Repeat the exercise five times, then change legs and repeat it five times on the other side (3b).

exercise 4

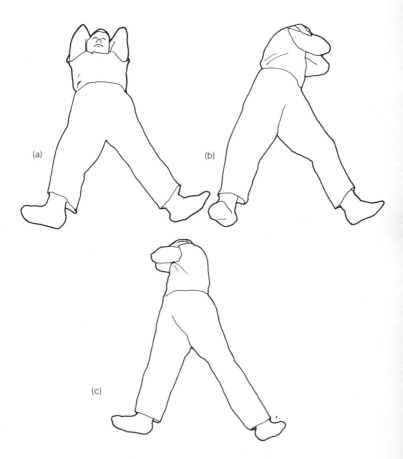

Lie on your back with your legs wide apart. Clasp your hands behind your neck and, keeping your legs stationary, roll your upper trunk first to one side (4a), then to the other (4b). Repeat the exercise, gently and rhythmically, ten times.

exercise 5

Sit on the floor with your left leg crossed over your right one. Move your right arm across your body and past the left knee, and rest it on the floor. Place your left hand on the floor behind you, about 15 centimetres (6 inches) away from your body. Use your left hand and arm to twist your body and head gently around until you are looking behind you. Hold this position for about ten in-breaths. *Do not force the twisting motion, and avoid sneezing or coughing while in this position, as both could be detrimental.*

exercise 6

(a)

(b)

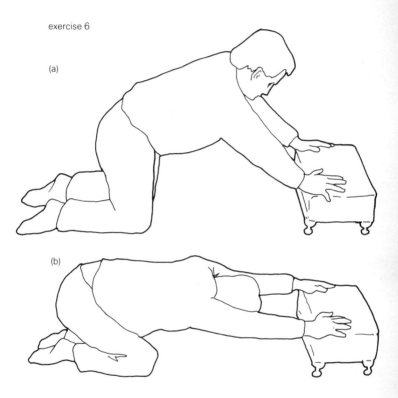

Kneel on the floor, and place your hands on a low foot-stool positioned about 20 centimetres (8 inches) beyond your head (6a). Keeping your arms straight, move your body downwards and backwards until your buttocks are almost resting on your heels (6b). Pause for a moment, then move forwards and upwards to regain your starting position. Repeat the exercise three or four times.

CHAPTER NINE

NECK AND SHOULDER PROBLEMS

Lesions Found in the Neck

Neck tension is an increasingly common affliction in modern society. When examining patients' necks, osteopaths frequently come across pain, tenderness, muscular knot-like contractions and some fibrous thickening; these tensions and tissue changes are so commonplace, in fact, that we are never surprised to find them even when the patient has come complaining of discomfort elsewhere in the body.

The cervical spine, made up of the vertebrae of the neck, is thought to be particularly susceptible to injury and strain due to the stress imposed upon it by the weight of the head, and its delicate, vital structures are especially prone to the wear and tear processes of ageing. Today's lifestyle does little to protect it. When I was a student, with not much money, I hitch-hiked a lift from a lorry driver to attend a seminar on osteopathy. During the journey I noticed that the driver's head was constantly jerking to and fro, buffeted by the movement of the lorry. I am never surprised now when drivers of heavy-goods vehicles attend my consulting rooms complaining of neck-ache! Driving any vehicle for long stretches can cause neck tension; so, of course, can sitting in a fixed position at a desk or telephone, particularly with the chin thrust forward. Emotional stress can be a contributory factor, since it causes people to tense up physically, particularly in the neck and shoulder area. Strains to the neck can also be brought about by musculoskeletal disorders elsewhere in the body.

The osteopathic theory is that stress in the spinal column can focus on certain specific areas of the spine; one such area in the neck lies between the third and fifth cervical bones. The reasons for this are thought to be, firstly, that the third cervical bone is the smallest within the cervical column, and secondly because the curve formed by the cervical column in response to the stress of gravity and weight-bearing is centred on the fourth cervical bone. This is probably why degenerative changes such as osteoarthritis and spondylosis are commonly detected by X-ray examination in the lower cervical area.

Lesions in the neck can also give rise to a number of problems which you might not immediately associate with osteopathic treatment. For example, mechanical problems in the upper cervical spine can also cause reflex disturbances producing symptoms of dizziness, blurred vision, unsteady balance and nausea. In this area the muscle spasm and contractions altering the mobility and alignment of the spine can impede the blood flow to the vertebral artery, which passes through openings in the cervical vertebrae, thus reducing the supply of blood and oxygen to the brain. Accurate diagnosis and careful osteopathic management can relieve or completely eliminate these symptoms, even when mild degenerative changes have taken place within the joints, as commonly arises from everyday wear and tear and the ageing process. Neck tension and pain can also be accompanied by symptoms of excessive fatigue, headaches and neuralgia-type pains at the back of the skull and in the face, shoulders, arms and hands, problems which often stem from cervical lesions.

Lesions in the joints at the top of the neck, just below the skull, produce many headache symptoms. People often consult me who have been suffering from daily headaches for some months, and are living on aspirins or similar medication. They are extremely grateful when, as a result of correcting the mechanical disturbances, the headaches subside and they can enjoy life again. Of course, not all headaches are produced by osteopathic lesions, and the osteopath must be aware of other possible causes during his examination. But a very high percentage of them can be eliminated when the cervical lesion causing them is reduced.

Apart from tension headaches, probably one of the most common complaints arising from lesions in the neck is pain radiating across the top of the shoulder and down into the arm, with sensations of pins and needles in the fingers. These symptoms can be the result of osteopathic lesions in the lower neck area.

Through clinical experience and research, osteopaths have found that cervical lesions can contribute to a myriad of symptoms and conditions, including insomnia, depression, conjunctivitis, laryngitis and chronic recurrent throat disorders, chronic recurrent rhinitis (cold in the head), sinusitis, tinnitus and torticollis.

Torticollis

This condition is sometimes called a wry-neck: the head and neck are twisted and pulled to one side by spasm and shortening of the muscles at the side of the neck. Most cases of torticollis are considered to be congenital, caused through trauma at birth leading to maldevelopment and a permanent shortening of the muscles; in these cases osteopathy can do nothing, and in extreme cases the only option is surgery.

However, there is also a condition termed 'acquired torticollis'; the pain this produces can be one of the worst resulting from muscle spasm, but it is usually amenable to osteopathic treatment. It sometimes results from a trauma, perhaps a jolt to the head, or turning the head sharply. More often, sufferers report that they awoke with the problem either during the night or in the morning; they have probably either made a violent twisting movement during sleep, or have been lying with the head in an awkward position, causing a prolonged stretching of one side of the neck muscles; even sleeping in a draught can cause torticollis.

I also believe that an infection in the neck area can contribute to this condition, when the already congested and irritated lymphatic and blood vessels could create reflex spasms of the muscles. Yet another factor can be emotional stress. I have found that many children suffering from this acute condition are under some kind of stress – it often afflicts them around school examination time. Acute torticollis is fairly common in children, usually as a result of the kind of factors already mentioned, but on rare occasions it may be the first sign of rheumatoid arthritis, or even the result of malformation of the joints in the upper neck.

The osteopath is fully aware of these possibilities, and here X-ray examination is a valuable aid to diagnosis.

Fortunately, when osteopathic treatment is administered in good time, torticollis can normally be alleviated very quickly. The aim of treatment at the acute stage is to reduce the inflammatory congestion and muscle spasm in order to prevent the complications of a chronic condition, and to release any osteopathic lesion which may be contributing to the spasm. The osteopath will usually advise applying cold packs to help decongest the irritated neck muscles, and soft-tissue manipulation and gentle passive motion techniques can help relax the muscle spasm. The osteopath will avoid using any forceful techniques or methods which may irritate the condition further. The functional manipulative methods (described in Chapter 5) are also of benefit here; they are gentle, efficient, and in no way unpleasant for the patient.

Whiplash Injuries

The most common cause of this type of injury is involvement in a motor vehicle collision, when the impact of the car behind causes the head to be jerked rapidly backwards and then forwards. Possible after-effects are pain, both at the front and the back of the neck, neuralgic pains in the shoulders, arms and hands, visual disturbances, dizziness, and headaches. In addition, a large number of patients have reported bouts of depression for the first time in their lives, or other psychological effects such as irritability, or even bouts of aggression.

The extent of the damage will of course vary. In extreme cases vertebrae have been known to be fractured, and ligaments torn and ruptured; such cases are obviously best seen by an orthopaedic surgeon. Most people who consult osteopaths for whiplash injuries have been to hospital first, and the majority will have had X-rays of the neck to rule out fractures.

Where there is no fracture, there is still usually damage to the ligaments, tendons, muscles, nerves and circulatory systems, and a disturbance of the mechanical mobility not only in the joints of the neck but also of the skull and sacrum. Many people suffering these less serious injuries – which are none-the-less painful and incapacitating – are given medically prescribed muscle relaxants, pain-killers and collars. These can help the ligaments, muscles and nerves to heal, but by themselves they are usually not enough; injuries to the tissues need other, complementary treatments for complete and satisfactory healing.

I am convinced that osteopathy not only helps the body to heal, but can also speed up the healing process. In addition, the osteopath's caring touch and personal communication with his patient can be very psychotherapeutic for any psychological after-effects.

Many whiplash victims continue to suffer from symptoms long after their accident, despite medical treatment; many, in fact, never really fully recover. I believe that this is because the *total* effect of the injury has not been treated. In the acute injury stage an osteopath will treat the whole spine; starting with the sacrum, he will then work on any lesions in the lumbar spine and then on the thoracic spine, in that order. Obviously, at the acute stage the neck is painful to touch and move; releasing the lesions further down the spine helps to reduce the tension in the muscles and ligaments, enabling the body's healing mechanisms to focus at the main site of the injury. At this stage it is definitely necessary to wear a collar to support the neck, but with successful osteopathic treatment this can be dispensed with very quickly.

X-rays are not only of value in ruling out fractures and any other serious pathology which result from extreme force; in severe cases they can also assist the osteopath in his diagnosis of any restricted mobility changes that have taken place after the injury has been sustained. These mobility X-rays are taken with the patient's head and neck bent first forwards and then backwards, so that the osteopath can note restricted areas from the arc thus formed. After successful manipulation, a further mobility X-ray can be taken to show that these restricted areas have been eliminated.

Once the very acute stage has passed, the structures and tissues of the neck can tolerate more localized handling. The osteopath can then apply gentle soft-tissue and passive motion techniques to help drain and reduce the congested tissues, and relieve spasm in the muscles. He can also give gentle intermittent traction to the head and neck, to stretch the muscles and release minor compressions of the joints. This in turn can help relieve neuralgia-type pains in the arms and shoulders, which are commonly experienced with this injury. The osteopath may also recommend Vitamin B therapy, which has proved useful in reducing this type of severe neuralgic arm pain.

There is no place for indiscriminate 'neck-popping' in the osteopathic management of the whiplash. The osteopath is concerned with the overall management of the injury; this will include attention to the cranium, or skull. Osteopaths believe and accept the theory that microscopic movements can take place between the sutures (joints) of the skull. The force of the impact in a whiplash injury affects not only the neck, but the whole spinal column, including the sacrum and the cranial bones. Symptoms indicating cranial bone disturbances are dizziness, certain visual problems, tinnitus, depression and facial pain. Osteopaths cannot stress enough the importance of treating the whole body in these types of injury. We are never surprised when patients report disappointing results following treatment to the neck alone.

CARING FOR YOUR NECK

- Respect your neck at all times, for it needs looking after from the moment you learn to stand. The upper part of the neck is a major control centre for the body, and also a major focal point for the central nervous system. Remember that all the tissues in the rest of the body depend on a normal flow of the nervous system from the brain as it passes through the neck.
- Do not tilt your chin forward and up. This can impede the flow of the circulatory and nervous sytems.
- Do not rest the telephone between your shoulder and ear while in conversation; over a period of time this can create an imbalance in the neck muscles.
- Do not continually jerk your head to flick your hair out of your eyes; you can run the risk of causing an osteopathic lesion in the neck.
- Do not sit or sleep in draughts at any time.

- Avoid sleeping on your stomach, to prevent prolonged turning of the head on one side.
- If you constantly wake up with a stiff neck, you may be using too many or too few pillows. The ideal number must depend on your build and the thickness of your pillows, but the important point is to keep the neck and head in as normal a position as possible, with your head neither pushed forward nor thrown back to 'kink' the neck.

CASE HISTORY (1)

A woman of forty consulted me for aching pains in her neck, the right side of her face and her right arm. This last symptom was made worse by even mild pressure, like wearing a heavy coat. She was also suffering from frequent headaches, and on occasions her facial pain was accompanied by a feeling of pins and needles.

She told me she had had these symptoms for as long as five or six years. Medical examination at her local hospital had found nothing abnormal, though after some X-rays had been taken of her neck she was told there was some arthritis present. When I examined her I found that her neck was very tense, and osteopathic lesions were present at C2–5 levels (the second to fifth cervical vertebrae). I also found tension restriction and tenderness in other areas of her spine, and duly recorded all these on her case sheet. I took her blood pressure, which was within normal limits.

I devoted most of the first treatment to the cervical region, releasing the muscle tension and mobilizing the restrictions I found. During this process I discovered that the second cervical vertebra, known as the axis, was the 'key lesion', which meant that reducing it would greatly relieve the restriction and tension in her entire neck. I treated this vertebra with a gentle, precise adjustment to restore its physiological relationship with the rest of the cervical joints.

On her second visit a week later, my patient reported that her facial pain was a great deal better and she had had no headaches since her first treatment. She was feeling generally easier, though she still had an intermittent aching and throbbing pain in her right arm. I used this second visit to re-examine the cervical spine, where there was a slight restriction at the fifth cervical level; this I released by gentle manipulation. I also took the opportunity to release the other spinal tensions and restrictions, to aid full recovery and help prevent the neck tensions from returning.

Further weekly visits were needed fully to correct her spinal problems and alleviate her symptoms to a very comfortable level. As her X-rays showed signs of wear and tear, probably due to an earlier injury to the neck, a complete cure was not possible, but as long as she comes for treatment every four to six weeks, this level of comfort can be maintained.

CASE HISTORY (2)

A man of thirty-two consulted me for tension pains in the neck, accompanied by headaches and dizziness, which had flared up some four or five weeks earlier. X-rays had been taken of the upper cervical spine, which showed nothing out of the ordinary. There was no immediate history of any injury to the neck, although my patient did recall falling very heavily during sports as a teenager, which had left him with a headache for a couple of days.

Although his X-rays had proved 'negative', I examined these, too. Osteopaths look at X-rays rather differently from radiologists. Radiologists look for important factors such as bone disease and structural bone faults, but osteopaths will, among other things, observe the symmetry of the facets linking each vertebra. In this case, I could see that the first cervical vertebra, known as the atlas, was held in a twisted position upon the axis below it. This mechanical fault I assessed as the cause of the young man's problems. It is possible that this originated with his fall as a teenager, but there is no way of being sure of this.

I found muscular tension in the upper part of his neck, and light pressure on this area with my fingers caused him a good deal of discomfort. In addition, his movement was restricted to one side when he turned his head, a common finding with this sort of problem.

Osteopaths are extremely careful when giving specific adjustments to this vulnerable area, and over the last few years they have developed manipulative techniques and testing procedures which ensure safety and avoid imposing any undue stress.

In this case, mobilizing the restricted area proved to be quite simple, requiring only the minimum of force. Sometimes the body seems to be waiting just for that little extra help, which the osteopath can give, to correct itself. This was one of those times; the manipulation was successful and I did not have to repeat it on later visits. For complete recovery, on this occasion and on later visits, I also gave my patient inhibitory soft-tissue manipulation and releasing techniques to alleviate tensions in the small deep muscles just below the skull.

CASE HISTORY (3)
A man of twenty-six consulted me complaining of a whole host of symptoms: dizziness, headaches, neck pain, aching across the shoulders, pain in the upper left arm, and intermittent pins and needles in the fingers of his left hand. He also complained of feelings of nausea, bouts of depression and loss of concentration.

All these symptoms had started up after he had been running along a beach carrying three sun-beds on his head, when he experienced a sharp jolt in his neck region, followed by dizziness and what he described as 'a funny feeling in the head'. That afternoon he felt an aching pain in his neck which increased in intensity as the day went on. The two friends he was with insisted that he should go to the local hospital casualty unit. He was X-rayed that same day, but the hospital could find nothing seriously wrong and advised him to see his own GP when he returned from holiday. This he did, and was prescribed pain-killers, but they did not provide lasting relief.

The trauma had occurred six or seven weeks before our consultation, and he had been suffering with all these problems ever since.

Examining his neck, I found that his general mobility was restricted in all directions, and trying to move his head and neck past the point of restriction was painful. Holding his head in certain positions increased the neck and arm pain and brought on the pins and needles in his hand.

Because of the pain and muscle tension I could give only minimal treatment to his neck on this first visit, and concentrated on relaxing the spinal tissues. Sometimes in such cases the osteopath needs to gain the patient's confidence on the first visit, by making it clear that he is not going to use harsh or rough movements, will not force anything, and will not cause the patient pain beyond his tolerance. Knowing he will be treated as gently as possible helps the patient to relax, and prevents nervousness and tension during subsequent visits; this in turn makes it easier for the osteopath to treat him.

I followed this up with treatments on consecutive days; on the third treatment the muscle spasm was greatly reduced and his neck movements were much easier. By this time he was much more relaxed, which made it easier for me to examine his neck. On this occasion I found a definite osteopathic lesion of the third cervical vertebra; I gently manipulated this, and it responded well. From this point on, the young man quickly made a full recovery.

Shoulder Problems

The shoulder is a ball and socket joint; it is capable of a wide range of movement in three planes, but this range of mobility takes its toll in the form of many shoulder joint problems. The humerus, the long bone of the upper arm, ends in a rounded shape which fits into a hollow known as the glenoid cavity. The depth of this cavity is really not sufficient for the head of the humerus, which makes the joint very susceptible to stresses and strains. The tendons, which attach the muscles to the bones, help to stabilize the shoulder joint; but in the shoulder they are constantly involved in movement and can very often become stressed, strained or injured.

Many people suffering with shoulder pain and disability don't realize that an osteopath could help them. This is a great pity, since osteopathy can be an effective form of treatment for many shoulder joint problems.

The great majority of these problems are caused by injury. One of the commonest ways to damage your shoulder is to fall with one arm outstretched, so that the force is transmitted through the hand and arm into the shoulder joint. This type of injury can also disturb the upper thoracic and lower cervical spinal areas, which can then also be involved in the pain and disability. Osteopaths will always examine these areas when dealing with shoulders, as they know that mechanical derangements here can upset nerves and blood vessels, impeding normal circulatory flow to the shoulder and arm. Another trauma or injury that upsets the shoulder joint mechanism is a direct impact to the point of the shoulder, from a blow or a fall.

But trauma is not the only cause of shoulder disabilities; constantly straining the area by repeated use of the arm can affect the structural integrity of the ligaments, tendons and muscles. On many occasions osteopaths have found that what has previously been diagnosed as 'bursitus' (an inflammation of the bursa, which is a small sac containing fluid that becomes inflamed due to injury or excessive pressure) is actually a strain of the joint mechanism which will respond favourably to osteopathic treatment.

As with any other condition, accurate diagnosis is extremely important. Pain in the shoulder region can be referred from a disease of the heart or lungs, and a differential diagnosis must be made to rule out this possibility.

The Frozen Shoulder Syndrome

The term 'frozen shoulder' is normally used when someone presents with a shoulder most of whose movements are limited in all directions; it is not a specific diagnosis, since there can be a variety of causes for the condition. It has been said that it takes about six months to develop and a year to eighteen months to go of its own accord. However, I have found that osteopathic treatment usually speeds up the recovery time, prevents muscle wastage through disuse, and very quickly controls the pain – long before full mobility is restored. Patients are very thankful for this, particularly those who have spent many nights awake with pain, and are enabled to get a good night's sleep.

Frozen shoulder syndrome is experienced by many people in their late fifties who develop stiff, painful shoulders, even without injury. In these cases the osteopath looks for evidence of the degenerative changes that can come as we grow older; he can often feel and hear a grating sensation where the tendons and joint surfaces have worn, while these patients normally complain of pain from the shoulder spreading down the side or front of the arm. They may well find it extremely difficult to move and use the arm, even to comb or brush their hair or wash their necks, or put a hand in a hip pocket.

Shoulder problems may also be accompanied by symptoms and signs of muscle wasting, dry skin, cold, clammy hands with discoloration, and also pains in the arm and hand with pins and needles and numbness. Many of these symptoms are worse at night when the person lies on the affected side, so this is obviously best avoided.

Although patients may only complain of discomfort in the shoulder and arm, the osteopath will rarely examine the shoulder girdle alone. He will normally first examine the patient's overall posture, noting the presence of any pelvic or spinal irregularities. This is because, as osteopaths are aware, the muscles of the shoulder region have wide and varied origins. They are attached to the base of the skull, the spinal column itself, the rib cage, the pelvis, the clavicles (collar bones) and the scapulae (shoulder blades). So a disturbance in any of these areas can be associated with shoulder dysfunctions. The osteopath, as always, thinks of the body as an integrated unit, in which mechanical disturbances in one part can affect the function in other areas.

Once the postural analysis has been assessed, the osteopath will examine the mobility of the shoulder joint itself, noting the restricted movements. He will then palpate for localized tissue contraction and tender nodules around the joint. He will carefully examine the function and alignment of the clavicle, or collar bone; lesions of this bone can often be responsible for pain and disability in the shoulder. Next, he will examine and feel the tissues and freedom of motion in the neck and the region of the spine between the shoulder blades, and will also give close attention to the upper rib cage. From here he will check the mobility of the rest of the spine and pelvis, noting any related problems. Sometimes X-rays may be needed to check for arthritic disorders and calcium deposits; they are also useful in ruling out fractures if the patient has suffered a fall or heavy blow.

On occasions a tendon may have been torn or ruptured, in which case the patient sometimes reports hearing a snapping sound on reaching out or lifting with the arm. In degenerative shoulders this can happen with a relatively minor force, but in normal shoulders it takes quite a lot of force to rupture a tendon. A clinical sign and test for suspected ruptured tendons is known as the 'drop arm test': the patient is asked to lift the arm out to the side and then lower it slowly. If there is a tear, the patient will not be able to lower it smoothly, and the arm will usually drop of its own accord. These cases are best referred to an orthopaedic surgeon for repair of the tendon.

Osteopaths usually carry out other clinical tests, including checking the tendon reflexes in the arm, checking for sensation loss over certain areas of the skin, and a check of the lymph nodes in the axilla (the arm-pit). (The lymph nodes which form part of the lymphatic system are found scattered throughout the body, usually in groups. They can become enlarged and tender, and are useful in diagnosing the site of an infection.) This thorough examination is necessary to find out whether osteopathy is indicated, or whether the patient should be referred for more appropriate treatment elsewhere.

Once the osteopath is satisfied with his findings, he will embark on treatment. Firstly, and very importantly, he uses his thumbs and fingers to release all muscular contractions; this is not usually unpleasant – rather the reverse, in fact, as afterwards the patient will experience greater freedom of movement and less pain in the shoulder and arm. The next step is for the osteopath to release any restriction and malalignment of the clavicle. The clavicle forms two important joints, and if these are lesioned they must be corrected to restore normal function and use to the shoulder and arm.*

The osteopath may also use passive motion techniques on the shoulder to increase mobility. Using these techniques he will move the shoulder joint rhythmically in several directions, always

* While on the subject, I feel it is a great pity that many hospitals have given up the figure-of-eight strapping technique for fractures of the clavicle; this form of strapping helps the bone to unite and heal better, without leaving the egg-shaped deformity that can be produced when a lesser strapping is used.

being careful to keep the movements within the patient's level of pain tolerance.

The osteopath will also give some attention to the neck and the upper spine between the shoulder blades, where most people with shoulder problems also experience some stiffness, aching and tension. Lesions in these areas can produce sensations of tingling in the arm and hand, and coldness in the hand, symptoms which are usually greatly relieved once these lesions are released. Releasing upper rib restriction also helps, especially when the arm feels heavy and there are signs of skin discoloration; this will remove pressure from the point known as the thoracic outlet or inlet, where many nerves, blood vessels and tubes pass through the skeletal framework to supply the neck, chest, arm and hand. If no specific lesions are found, the osteopath will give some soft-tissue manipulation to aching, tense muscles in these areas.

Forceful treatment should never be given to frozen shoulder conditions in an attempt to speed recovery. Most cases will eventually respond favourably to osteopathy, although, as always, the recovery time will depend on the severity and duration of the problem, and the patient's age. As a rough guide, osteopaths often find that full recovery takes about a third of the time for which the problem has existed. Both patient and osteopath may need to be patient, especially at times when the treatment reaches a plateau stage, with the condition getting no worse but apparently not improving either.

Despite the need for time and patience, I do feel that osteopathy should rate as first choice of treatment for the frozen shoulder syndrome.

EXERCISES FOR THE FROZEN SHOULDER PATIENT
Patients can assist in their recovery by practising any exercises the osteopath recommends. The following are useful as a general guide:

● To improve shoulder mobility, a good exercise is to stand bent slightly forward, with the involved arm hanging down; then swing the arm to and fro across the body like a pendulum. Still in this position, the arm can also be swung in circles, clockwise and then anti-clockwise.

- Another exercise I recommend is to slowly 'walk' both hands up a wall or door. You can put a mark on the door showing how far you can reach at the start, and measure progress during the course of treatment.
- Hold the arms out at right angles, bent at the elbows, and swing the arms backwards and forwards from the elbows. This also helps the shoulder to regain mobility.
- It can also be helpful to extend the arms, palms up, and make small circles with the hands.

CASE HISTORY

Mrs B., a forty-six-year-old dental receptionist, came to me suffering with a severe so-called frozen shoulder, with pain spreading downwards from her shoulder to her upper arm. She complained that since her shoulder had been bad she had also suffered neck pain and stiffness from time to time. The onset of her problems was roughly six months before she came to see me. She believed she might have strained her shoulder while lifting something out of her car, but could not be absolutely certain.

The movement of her shoulder was grossly limited. She had difficulty in raising her arm to the front and side, and found it impossible to reach behind her back. She remarked that it was lucky that it was her left shoulder and arm that were affected, as she was right-handed. The pain was generally aching in character, but could become sharp on movement, and it was affecting her sleep, as it was extremely painful to lie on her left arm.

During my examination I found various muscular tensions and tender areas around her shoulder, neck and upper back and ribs, with the associated osteopathic lesions, so I gave specific treatment to these areas. After three treatments there was no visible improvement, but after the fourth she noticed a reduction in pain and could move the shoulder a little more. At this stage I prescribed exercises for her to do every day.

As I commented earlier, shoulder problems can take a long time to treat, but patience pays off in the end. After twelve treatments over a three-month period, Mrs B.'s pain was much better and movement was easier, but there was still some restriction. After another ten treatments – totalling nearly six months in all – her shoulder and arm were completely pain-free, and movement was near normal.

CHAPTER TEN

ARTHRITIS AND RHEUMATISM:

CAN OSTEOPATHY HELP?

Rheumatism is a non-specific term often used to describe general aches and pains; generally it indicates that the patient is suffering from some kind of arthritic disorder. Even the word 'arthritis' is used in a very broad sense, to describe pain in the joints and muscles.

Arthritis is one of the oldest diseases – or more accurately, groups of diseases – known to mankind, and still one of the most feared. In the Natural History Museum in London you can see skeletons of the spinal column dating back four thousand years, which show arthritic bony spurs and evidence of arthritic fusion of the spinal joints. Throughout the ages many of our ancestors suffered from arthritic pain and disability, and probably struggled through life hopefully taking the potions and medicines popular in their time; but no real cure has so far been found.

There are numerous types of arthritis, but the two most common and best known are rheumatoid arthritis and osteoarthritis.

Rheumatoid Arthritis is the most painful and crippling of the two, and the most difficult to manage and treat. It normally affects several joints at once: the fingers, knuckles and wrists are common targets for this disease. As well as pain, there is heat, redness and swelling at these sites, and because it is a systematic disease, it affects the whole person, producing fatigue, weakness and stiffness throughout the body. It attacks more women than men, although neither sex and no age-group is safe from it.

Osteoarthritis is usually a good deal less serious and incapacitating than rheumatoid arthritis; the pain can vary from mild or moderate to severe. It is also known as 'degenerative joint disease', as it chiefly occurs with advancing age. Unlike rheumatoid arthritis it may affect only one joint, the most susceptible being the weight-bearing joints, the spine, hips, knees and ankles. It is rarely accompanied by inflammatory signs of heat and redness at the joints.

Two other arthritis conditions which osteopaths are called upon to treat are ankylosing spondylitis and spondylosis.

Ankylosing Spondylitis primarily affects the spine, and is found to be more common in men than women. The onset starts early, normally before the age of thirty. As with most forms of arthritis, the cause of this disorder is unknown. It starts either in the lower back area (to be precise, within the sacro-iliac joints) or in the cervical joints of the neck. Wherever it starts, it spreads progressively to affect the whole spine, causing the joints to fuse, which makes the whole spinal column extremely rigid. This rigidity can also affect the chest, so that it cannot expand fully when a deep breath is taken.

Osteopathic treatment can help people suffering from this condition, although it is not wise to give any treatment during the active inflammatory stage. Once this has subsided, appropriate manipulation can be given to try to maintain or improve the mobility of the spine and chest. This can be accomplished with soft-tissue and passive motion techniques, providing a complete fusion of the vertebrae has not taken place.

Spondylosis is sometimes confused with osteoarthritis of the spine. Basically it consists of degeneration of the discs and vertebrae resulting from wear and tear. It is frequently detected by X-ray, and a very high percentage of people over fifty show some evidence of spondylosis. It can start with an injury, often many years before, or with mechanical stresses placed upon the spine such as osteopathic lesions and poor posture.

A large number of people whose spinal X-rays show some evidence of the wear and tear signs that characterize this condition may not be complaining of any pain at all, although they may be experiencing some stiffness. Others, however, suffer both stiffness and pain, and it is this last which brings them to seek treatment and advice.

Spondylosis responds quite favourably to carefully applied osteopathic manipulation, which can both relieve pain and improve mobility.

The Possible Causes of Arthritis

Before the osteopath embarks on any treatment, he needs to be aware of the possible causes of the patient's condition. In the case of arthritis, these can include any one or a combination of the following:

1. Hereditary factors which may predispose the individual to these complaints
2. Inborn deficiencies in the immune or defensive mechanisms
3. Trauma, including osteopathic lesions
4. Endocrine (glandular) imbalance
5. Bodily pollution
6. Emotional stress

Looking at this list it is clear that whatever therapy is chosen to treat arthritic disorders, a broad therapeutic approach to the whole problem is needed. Although there is so far no known cure, many people have found considerable relief of pain by various means. These include orthodox medicaments, homoeopathic and herbal remedies, vitamins and minerals, special dietary regimes, medical hypnosis, acupuncture, and manipulative methods such as chiropractic and osteopathy.

Before going any further, let me quote what the founder of osteopathy, Dr Andrew Still, wrote on the subject in the late 1800s:

I have long since been satisfied that all the so-called rheumatic suffering comes from the chemical action of poisonous fluids that should have been normally excreted from the system. I think it is an effect which is the result of impure compounds carried to and deposited in the vicinity of the joints of any part of the body.

When any part of the body receives a jolt by a fall, a mental or physical shock or wound, many kinds of abnormal compounds and fluids are produced, confused, brought together and circulate in the system. If these abnormal fluids are not returned on time, but are deposited in the membranes – congestion, fermentation or decomposition of the impure chemical compound follows.

When venous blood has been obstructed and retained in the region of the spinal cord and of the cerebellum by impingement or muscle contractures operating to hold the upper cervical bones out from their normal positions, we have a condition that will result in rheumatism. To stop the return of blood from above the articulation of the atlas with the occiput until stagnation sets up in the venous blood will result in heat and inflammation.

Constriction and stoppage of blood at this place long enough will form poisonous compounds that take the place of healthy nerve fluid which should come from the brain. This poisonous fluid taken up by the pneumogastric and cardiac nerves is soon distributed to the entire body and this delivery of impure fluids results in a stagnation in the heart, liver, kidneys and the entire excretory system. Here the mystery of rheumatism disappears. This applies to both acute and chronic rheumatism. Open the gates and let the bondman go free. I have worked accordingly and the results have been good. (Still, 1910, pp. 369–73.)

Osteopaths today would not make such extensive claims as the founder of osteopathy. There is no established evidence to suggest that osteopathic lesions of the upper neck joints, or for that matter any other area of the spine can *cause* arthritis. However, osteopathic lesions cannot definitely be ruled out as a *contributory* factor. And although osteopathy cannot cure arthritis it may, along with other treatments, help the body to establish a better chemical balance which improves the general health and in rheumatoid arthritis may therefore assist in the bringing about of remission.

Once he has established a diagnosis of arthritis, the osteopath's first step is to explain the possible causes to the patient. It is important to give the patient a full understanding of his or her condition, as this will help them to cooperate with their treatment regime. Many people stop treatment once their pain and discomfort have been relieved, only to find them returning after a short time. They must accept that whatever therapy they choose will be of a long-term nature: pain must be understood as the *result* of the condition, not the cause. The basis of any treatment is to try to stop the degenerative process and even to reverse it by aiding the body to programme itself for reconstruction. How do we try to achieve this?

Nutrition

Firstly, the patient's diet must be looked at. A diet that does not care for or consider the body's eliminative system, or for that matter the body in general, is taking the patient on the road to disaster. In Chapter 6, I introduced the problem of chemical overload and described how the body becomes polluted by impurities from bad nutrition. One possible effect of this is that, unless the imbalance is rectified, the body's elimination system will become overloaded and, given time, a build-up of the impurities may bring about an arthritic condition.

The osteopath will not recommend an identical nutritional programme to every patient, but will design one for each individual's needs. However, natural, fresh foods unpolluted by chemicals are usually the order of the day – although, unfortunately, it is difficult to obtain high quality foods free of chemical sprays. There are also some specific foods which should *always* be avoided. These include foods high in sugar – cakes, sweets, chocolates, biscuits, ice cream and soft drinks, for example. White flour, dairy products and highly processed foods should also be avoided or kept to the very minimum. The osteopath will not only advise the patient what not to eat, but also – most importantly – should provide a list of the foods that *can* be eaten.

One reason for following a natural diet is to keep bowel movements regular, as most arthritics have problems with elimination. Normally functioning bowels allow the body to rid itself of unwanted waste materials from the foods we eat, helping to keep the system free of impurities and preventing the build-up of chemical poisons. The nutritional programme may also be designed to help the patient lose weight, for overweight is a common enemy of the arthritic. Excess weight puts strain and stress upon joints which traumatizes them, and may contribute to arthritis.

The Endocrine System is a very important consideration when dealing with arthritis. Endocrine glands are responsible for the production of hormones, which they secrete directly into the bloodstream, producing widespread effects of various kinds throughout the body.

Hitherto unknown hormones and their actions within the body are constantly being discovered, and of all our bodily systems, the endocrine system is the one about which the least is known. To give you an idea of its complexity, the pituitary gland, which forms a part of it, is known to have at least fifty different functions that we know of – and it seems likely that there are still more to be discovered!

Any imbalance in hormone secretion can set up a variety of problems, including arthritic conditions. So, when dealing with an arthritic patient the osteopath will look very closely at the areas of the spine that, when lesioned, can impede nerve and blood flow to the endocrine glands.

In America, osteopaths carried out a structural examination on five hundred patients who had been diagnosed as having either osteoarthritis or rheumatoid arthritis, to find out whether they showed a particular pattern of osteopathic lesions. It was discovered that in fact three spinal areas showed a high incidence of lesions: the occipito-atlantal joint, the thoraco-lumbar junction, and the lumbosacral joint.

A number of osteopaths believe the two bones at the top of the neck which form the occipito-atlantal joint, when lesioned in a malaligned, restricted and tense state, may indirectly impair normal nerve and blood supply to the pituitary gland. They also believe that loss of motion between the spinal segments of the tenth thoracic and second lumbar vertebrae, known as the thoraco-lumbar junction, can impede normal blood flow to the adrenal glands. These glands are second only to the pituitary gland in the number of different hormones they secrete. In fact, the pituitary and adrenal glands are in close communication with each other: the pituitary secretes a fluid known as adreno-cortico-trophic-hormone (known as ACTH) which stimulates the adrenals to secrete cortisone. Cortisone may not cure arthritis, but it is known that cortisone can help the pain and inflammation caused by the disease.

Treating Arthritic Conditions

Some arthritic patients, who may be in considerable pain, are nervous of consulting osteopaths for fear the treatment will be painful. And some are discouraged by their doctors, who doubt the benefits and safety of osteopathic treatment. I can understand this, for many of them visualize the osteopath twisting and cracking joints forcibly – which would certainly do the patient no good! But it should be clear by now that many osteopathic techniques are extremely gentle and painless. If some doctors are still unaware of this, it may to some degree be due to a lack of communication between the two professions. This is very sad, for although arthritis cannot be cured, numbers of sufferers can have the quality of their lives greatly improved, with reduced pain and increased mobility.

What, then, can a person expect when consulting an osteopath for an arthritic disorder? He or she should expect to be given a thorough consultation, followed by a thorough examination of posture and the musculoskeletal system. The osteopath may also need to include X-rays and specific laboratory tests to confirm his clinical diagnosis, and treatment will obviously depend on his findings.

Rheumatoid Arthritis. Osteopaths have to be extremely cautious in dealing with the acute active phase of this disease; when there is much inflammation, swelling and pain even the mildest form of manipulative contact may provoke further inflammatory reaction in the joint. Diagnosis therefore has to include the exact joints involved, so that the osteopath can avoid any contact at these specific areas.

This does not mean, however, that the rheumatoid patient cannot be helped; far from it. The osteopath can play a very important role, and when correct management is employed improvement can usually be expected. Although he will not touch an inflamed joint, he can treat the areas above and below it, administering gentle techniques to maintain or enhance muscular tone, improve blood and nerve supply and preserve joint motion and function in these areas. Another important aspect of treatment is that the osteopath can identify osteopathic lesions and, when possible, obtain their release; this will reduce the mechanical stress of the body as a whole, improving overall bodily function.

Another totally painless technique is cranial osteopathy, which I will be describing more fully in Chapter 12. It has been found that gently compressing the skull improves the flow of the cerebrospinal fluid, which bathes and nourishes the brain and the central nervous system. This is believed to make the hormones, enzymes and nutrients it contains better available to the body; it can have remarkable effects in relieving the pain of both rheumatoid arthritis and osteoarthritis. (See case history, pages 166–7.)

John E. Upledger, DO, FAAO, an American osteopath, cites a case in his book *Craniosacral Therapy*, co-authored by Jon D. Vredevoogd, MFA (1983), when he treated a patient who had advanced rheumatoid arthritis – in fact the surgeons were at the stage of operating on both hips. When he started his treatment the patient was unable to walk and was confined to a wheelchair. Upledger used a combination of acupuncture, traditional osteopathy, cranial osteopathy and nutrition. A very important part of this treatment was the technique of gentle compression of the skull; Upledger taught this to a relative of the patient who carried it out daily. As Upledger explains, it is a harmless technique which speeds the removal of unwanted chemicals from the body, with none of the complications of anti-inflammatory drugs. The happy ending to this story is that the patient was relieved of his pain and helped to a near-complete remission of the disease without having to undergo surgery.

Most osteopaths will also play an important role by giving nutritional advice, as described above, and will also advise as to what supplements to take, if these seem to be required. In some cases they can be essential, as inflammatory diseases increase the body's requirements of vitamins and minerals.

I recognized the value of correct nutrition during my early experiences with rheumatoid arthritis. Several of my patients had been exploring the dietary factor for themselves, and told me that they had benefited from changing their diet. Since then, I have nearly always included a nutritional programme in the management of this disease, and I find that many people experience a considerable reduction in pain when they follow the nutritional programme that is right for them.

Another important factor is that the osteopath can also provide psychological support and reassurance. Although it has not been proved that emotional crises are a causative factor in arthritic conditions, osteopaths who deal with arthritic patients almost invariably discover that they are under some kind of severe stress, in addition to the pain and anxiety caused by the disease. A good example is a woman who told me that her rheumatoid arthritis had started nine years before, soon after she had suffered the shock of her daughter walking out of her life for good. Other patients often have marital or financial worries which may be creating or adding to stress reactions within their bodies. So you can see that to obtain positive results, not only must the practitioner treat holistically, it is also important for them to inspire the patient's confidence and trust: moral support can be a valuable aid in the healing process.

The osteopath can also advise on the patient's lifestyle and exercise. Patients frequently ask me whether they should keep on the move and ignore the pain, or whether they should rest. Rest is in fact a very important therapy for the inflammatory process which happens during this disease, and I personally always advise patients to rest totally for regular intervals during the course of each day; the length of these rest periods must vary according to each individual's need and the severity of the disease. But this doesn't mean that sufferers should allow themselves to become chairbound; some movement is essential to maintain muscular tone and joint function. This is where carefully applied osteopathic treatment, together with individually prescribed exercises, can be of great benefit.

Many rheumatoid arthritis patients find that medical drugs are effective in relieving pain. Osteopathy can be complementary to drug therapy, and many people benefit greatly from having the best of both forms of medicine. An advantage of having correct, non-forceful osteopathic as well as medical treatment is that over the course of time some patients are able to reduce their drug intake to a minimum. This should always be done under the guidance of the patient's doctor, and is yet another reason why the more communication there can be between the two professions, the better for the patient.

Osteoarthritis. Treatment will depend on individual cases, but as always, the osteopath will look at and may treat the patient as a whole, rather than simply the painful area. As an example, take someone with osteoarthritis of the knee joint. The osteopath may deem it necessary not only to give treatment locally to the knee with soft-tissue manipulation, passive motion techniques and perhaps some form of electrotherapy, but also to examine and treat other areas of the body which may have a mechanical and functional linkage; these include the foot, hip, pelvis, and spine. So never be surprised if, when you consult an osteopath, he proceeds to look at other areas of your body in addition to the painful joint. Again, the osteopath may give advice on nutrition and suitable exercises for the individual, and patients can do a good deal to help themselves in this way – as the first case history below shows.

I myself have treated many people with osteoarthritis and find that the treatment can often considerably reduce their pain. In addition, it improves mobility within the involved joint, for which patients are usually very grateful.

This improvement in symptoms is possibly due to the release of muscular tension and contraction and improved drainage of the fluids around the joints concerned. Once this level of improvement has been reached most people will need to visit the osteopath periodically to maintain it. Another good reason for continuing to attend at regular intervals is that very often the osteopath will find osteopathic lesions superimposed upon the arthritic joint: eliminating these further helps to reduce the pain and improve function at the joint involved.

So, yes, osteopathy can help. Although it cannot *cure* arthritic disease, along with other treatment regimes it can stop or slow down the degenerative process, and many of my arthritic patients say it helps to 'keep them going'. They often experience some relief of pain and improvement in mobility and, in addition, they feel generally better in themselves.

I also believe that osteopathic treatment, given in time, could prevent osteoarthritis from setting in, in cases where some injury or strain has set up a mechanical dysfunction within the joint. Unfortunately, people often do not get this kind of mechanical joint derangement treated soon enough; then, because of the resultant imbalance, the repetition of mild strains and traumas during daily living creates unnecessary wear and tear, culminating in arthritis.

CASE HISTORY (1)

A woman of fifty-six consulted me in desperation; she had become so stiff and immobile that she could only shuffle into my consulting-room on two sticks, her body bent forward, suffering from pain in her lower back, buttocks and both thighs. When she lay on her back she could not straighten her legs, and had to keep them semi-flexed.

Palpation of her hip joints and lower spine indicated that osteoarthritis was present. This was confirmed by X-rays, although to my surprise the arthritis was not as bad as I had expected from the clinical signs and symptoms she presented. I recommended that she consult an orthopaedic surgeon with a view to having hip replacements. However, she was not at all keen on this as she was afraid of operations, and she begged me to help her. I agreed to try, making it clear that osteopathy could not cure her condition and that I was not even sure that I could help.

I began treatment with her feet, and once I had achieved reasonable mobilization I worked upwards, attempting to release restrictions within the knee joints and muscular contractions of the thighs. I knew I could not mobilize the very rigid hip joints, so I bypassed them and worked on the soft-tissue contractions and joint dysfunctions of the pelvis and spine.

After six treatments, the pain in her lower back had become slightly easier, and she was able to stand more upright. However, her hip joints were as rigid as ever. I couldn't help noticing that my patient shuffled, with her feet splayed out, so I decided to spend the whole of the next treatment session showing her how to walk. I encouraged her to turn her feet slightly inwards and to take larger strides; I also showed her husband how it should be done, and asked him to keep an eye on how she walked. She agreed to practise by taking a daily walk; as she hadn't been outside her house for nearly a year, apart from her visits to me, this in itself was quite an achievement.

After coming to me for weekly treatments for nine months and carrying out these concentrated walking exercises at home, my patient was able to abandon her walking-sticks, though she still carried one over her arm, mainly to give her confidence. It was most rewarding for me when she and her husband told me that she was able to walk to her local shopping centre without pain for the first time in nearly two years, and was starting to enjoy life again.

She still has treatment periodically to maintain the level of improvement. Obviously, given the nature of her condition a complete cure cannot be effected, but she is still a very grateful patient.

CASE HISTORY (2)

Mr P., a sixty-year-old railway worker, consulted me for pain and stiffness in his lower back. This pain would also spread to the right hip and groin, and it was constant, ranging from an ache to sharp stabbing pains. The worst time was always first thing in the morning, and Mr P. would nearly always find it a struggle to put his socks on. These symptoms had been getting worse over the previous nine months, though they had been present in a milder form for at least five years.

Before coming to see me, Mr P. had consulted his doctor, who sent him for an X-ray, which showed that he had spondylosis of the lumbar spine. Osteopathic examination found his spine to be very rigid, with a lateral curvature. The hip joints appeared to be normal.

I treated him with soft-tissue manipulation, stretching and passive motion techniques, in order to improve the circulation and mobility of the lower back. I gave four treatments like this, which resulted in a vast improvement. Although Mr P. still suffered from a stiff lower back first thing in the morning, once he got going the stiffness and ache wore off and he was much more mobile and pain-free during the rest of the day. After another six treatments, the morning problems were greatly improved, and he was experiencing only occasional mild twinges.

Mr P. now attends once a month to maintain this improvement. On his last visit he told me how pleased he was to be feeling so much better.

CASE HISTORY (3)

Mr H. A. was forty-one years old, and had suffered from ankylosing spondylitis since his early twenties. When he came to see me he was in a very bad way, as the disease had progressed to its full extent. It had left him severely round-shouldered, with his head and neck jutting forward. His neck and spinal movements were rigid – so much so that he could not look up to the ceiling. Although he tried to exercise by swimming, he told me that he could not do the front crawl because he could not lift his head out of the water.

He had consulted me, not with the hope of a cure since he knew there was none, but with the hope that osteopathy might help with the constant ache he was getting around his neck and shoulders. He described this ache as a muscular soreness and tiredness; I was not surprised to find that his muscles felt like tightropes.

Soft-tissue manipulation was the only form of treatment I gave him, and I performed it with him sitting. My aim was to try to reduce the muscle tension and aching-type pain. Progress was slow, but after three months of weekly treatment he was noticing a significant reduction in pain. Mr H. A. now visits me every three to six weeks, according to his need, and although I cannot improve his spinal mobility, I am delighted to be of assistance in reducing his pain.

CASE HISTORY (4)

Mrs G., a housewife of thirty-nine, was suffering with rheumatoid arthritis, diagnosed by her doctor and hospital about one year before consulting me. She had severe joint pain and swelling in both hands and wrists, and to a lesser degree pain and stiffness in the elbows and knees. The stiffness was always worst in the mornings. Her doctor had prescribed non-steroid anti-inflammatory drugs which did help, but she found that they were beginning to upset her digestion and was wondering if other forms of more natural treatment could help her.

Examination of her spine revealed, in addition to her disease, that she had osteopathic lesions in the upper neck, mid-lower back region, and the sacrum. During the consultation, I recognized that she was under a lot of stress. She was running her own business, and because of this her dietary habits were appalling – she was living on junk foods for convenience.

I gave her some specific dietary advice, and recommended her to do the breathing and relaxation exercises described in Chapter Six. I treated her with cranial osteopathy and functional technique, a very gentle manipulative method, for her spine. Although there was no evidence of arthritis in the spine, I preferred this to more forceful techniques, which even performed with the utmost care and precision might cause painful reactions in this group of patients. I also applied interferential therapy locally to the affected joints, to help reduce the pain and swelling.

After four months of weekly treatment there was a vast improvement. Mrs G.'s wrists were no longer swollen, and she had been able to greatly reduce her drug intake. She kept to the recommended diet and practised the relaxation method, and after another four months of treatment she had reached a nearly total remission, apart from occasional mild pains. Since then she has attended periodically for check-ups and treatment, and has maintained this level of relief for just over two years now.

CHAPTER ELEVEN

OSTEOPATHY FOR SPECIFIC

PROBLEMS IN WOMEN AND CHILDREN

Women's lives make them particularly susceptible to back-ache: housework, pregnancy, standing at sinks and ironing boards, carrying children and heavy shopping can all take their toll on vulnerable spines. As well as benefiting from osteopathic treatment, women can take preventative measures, such as the relaxation and postural exercises already described; they can also help to prevent their children from growing up with similar problems.

In addition, there are some specifically female problems with which osteopathy can help. On numerous occasions women seeking help with back problems have been surprised to find that their whole body begins to function better after treatment. This is no accident since, as I have tried to emphasize throughout this book, osteopathy takes into account the whole structure and function of the person. For example, most women don't realize that osteopathy can help with painful periods; during my time in practice only two have come to me specifically for this problem. Yet a great many of my women patients have remarked that since having osteopathy their periods have been less painful.

Menstrual Problems

Dysmenorrhea, or painful menstruation, can be a problem for some women at the onset of their monthly menstrual cycle. Dysmenorrhea is different from pre-menstrual tension, which usually occurs between four to ten days before the period. The commonly recognized symptoms of pre-menstrual tension are tender breasts, abdominal bloating, changes of mood such as irritability and depression, and sometimes swelling of the feet and legs.

It is with dysmenorrhea that osteopathy appears to be most helpful. The symptoms usually start a couple of hours before the flow appears, varying from mild to intense lower abdominal pain, which may also radiate to the back and sometimes the legs. For the osteopath to help with this problem, he must first rule out any pathological cause within the pelvic organs. If the patient is suffering from primary dysmenorrhea – painful menstruation with no pathological cause – her history will show that the pain probably started with her first monthly cycles or a few years after this, and has continued ever since. This point is very helpful in making a diagnosis. However, if the osteopath is in any doubt, he will recommend the patient to get a definite diagnosis from a gynaecologist before starting any treatment.

Once a diagnosis of primary dysmenorrhea has been established, osteopathy can be of enormous benefit. Women who suffer painful periods are often found to have osteopathic lesions in the lower back and pelvic area, where nerves exit from the spinal cord to become a source of supply to the uterus. When these lesions exist, they irritate the nerves leading to the uterus, causing it to contract, which creates pain and discomfort.

The osteopath will begin treatment by asking the patient to lie face down and applying a firm steady pressure to the sacrum with both hands. This pressure helps to relax the irritated sacral nerves, which in turn will bring about a relaxation of the uterus, and is maintained for at least five minutes. After this, manipulative treatment will be given to the spinal and pelvic lesions present, in order to normalize their alignment and mobility, which will promote better nerve function and improved blood flow to the uterus.

Another technique that osteopaths employ in these cases is to apply pressure with both thumbs in the regions of the pubic symphysis joint, the joint formed by the two large pelvic bones which join one another at the lower front of the pelvis. This, like the pressure to the sacrum described above, can bring relief actually during painful menstruation. These techniques are simple enough for the osteopath to teach them to the patient's husband, relative or friend, who can then relieve the pain in both the lower abdomen and back when it is at its peak.

CASE HISTORY (1)

A young woman of twenty-five, who helped to run a local guest-house, came to me complaining of severe lower abdominal and back-pain at the start of each monthly cycle. On most occasions the pain was bad enough for her to have to go to bed with aspirins, and she was losing at least one or two days' work every month. She had consulted her GP, who diagnosed her problem as primary dysmenorrhea; he had explained the problem thoroughly to her and assured her that there was nothing seriously wrong. This had at least put her mind at rest. However, the only treatment the doctor could suggest was mild analgesics and bed rest; although this helped temporarily, the effect was only palliative, and over the past year or so the problem had seemed to be getting worse. She had decided to come to me because she had read somewhere that osteopathy could be helpful with painful menstruation.

When I examined her I found spinal lesions of the facet joints of the upper lumbar spine and a sacral torsion lesion (this condition is described in Chapter Eight). I gave manipulative treatment to these areas to restore joint alignment and mobility. I also taught her the pressure techniques to the sacrum and pubic symphysis joint, so that her husband could apply them as first aid during painful menstruation. And I also recommended her to practise the relaxation exercises (described in Chapter Six) at least once every day.

She came for ten treatments in all, and over the course of time the menstrual pain steadily lessened. On some occasions she would have no pain at all, and on others would only experience a mild pain. As a result of the treatment she no longer had to take to her bed and lose time from work.

CASE HISTORY (2)

A woman physiotherapist, aged twenty-six, consulted me for severe lower abdominal pain, back-pain and a tired, aching feeling in her legs. She told me that the onset of these pains always coincided with her monthly cycle and would make her feel 'rotten' for a few days. This would sometimes affect her work, as the pain disturbed her concentration. She had suffered with painful periods ever since they had first started. However, she had noticed that they had definitely become worse since she had been working as a physiotherapist, which involved a great deal of standing for long periods.

Through her work, she had attended a lecture given by an osteopath who mentioned that osteopathy could help painful menstruation, and she had decided to give it a try. I treated her once a week, in a similar manner to the patient described above. After three months she noticed a considerable improvement; I then continued to treat her fortnightly for another four months until complete relief was obtained.

CASE HISTORY (3)
In this case, as so often happens, the patient's painful menstruation cleared up in the course of other treatment. This young woman came to see me complaining of neck, shoulder and arm pain, after over-reaching to play an overarm badminton shot. I directed osteopathic manipulation not only to these regions, but also to the lower back and pelvis where I also found lesions in need of correction. After several treatments she was very pleased to report that her neck and arm pain were much better. She also asked whether osteopathy could affect menstrual pain as before the treatment she had always suffered with back-pain and lower abdominal cramp, but since having treatment she had noticed that her last two periods had been far less painful.

Pregnancy and Childbirth

While I have been writing this book, my wife has been expecting our second child. During this period she has found that by having frequent and regular osteopathic treatment she has not had to suffer the back-pain so many pregnant women complain of.

During pregnancy, as the baby develops and grows, the mother's posture and centre of gravity are altered by the increased frontal load, with the main postural change taking place during the last three months. In the normal lumbar spine there is a natural curve on a level with the waistline known as a lordosis; the increased forward weight caused by pregnancy causes an exaggeration of this lordotic curve, which can compress and place a strain upon the small joints of the low back, often giving rise to nagging low-back ache.

Earlier in this book I made the point that any woman should consider a visit to an osteopath as soon as she plans to start a family. I cannot stress too strongly the value of an osteopathic check-up at this early stage. I am certain that it would save many women much distress, both from low-back pain and from other areas of spinal tension and discomfort. This is because pre-existing osteopathic lesions, which may be giving such little trouble that they have been ignored, can be aggravated by the additional weight and postural tension of pregnancy. Pregnancy will obviously be much more enjoyable if these can be corrected in advance. If women develop back-ache during pregnancy it is possible to give them osteopathic treatment, using gentle methods such as functional techniques, but in my experience it is much easier to correct lesions beforehand and prevent the back-ache from occurring in the first place.

Another very common problem among pregnant women is heartburn: my wife was no exception. It may surprise you to know that osteopathy proved to be extremely helpful for this. I used a relatively simple technique, applying pressure with both thumbs to the upper and mid-thoracic spinal areas, located between the shoulder blades. As most women frequently get this problem while lying down, it can start up late at night; it is very useful for husbands to be taught how to apply this simple pressure so that relief is readily to hand.

Osteopathy can also be very helpful during the labour itself. In my own case, the hospital maternity staff were both caring and open-minded enough to allow me to help my wife through her labour and the delivery of our second child, so I know from experience how beneficial osteopathy can be in this situation. Of course, it is unusual for a woman to have her osteopath accompanying her to hospital! These days, however, many maternity hospitals encourage husbands to be present during the labour and birth, and osteopaths can show them beforehand how to carry out some simple massage-type techniques.

For example, the pain of the contractions can be eased by natural means: one method is to have the mother-to-be in a sitting position, and to apply pressure to the low-back and sacral area at the beginning of a contraction. In fact, osteopaths believe that – providing there are no complications – the woman should adopt a sitting position for most of the labour. In this position, the lumbar spine can be mobilized and the spine just above the lumbar area rotated; this helps to stimulate contractions naturally, preventing a long labour and promoting a normal delivery. As for what position is generally best for birth, the modern trend in hospitals is to advise the woman to adopt whatever position is most comfortable for her, and there should be no rigid rules about this. However, the sitting position does seem more natural as it allows gravity to play a natural part.

Cystitis

True cystitis is caused by an inflammation of the bladder, generally due to an infection or injury; although both sexes are subject to it, it is especially common in women. The symptoms can be agonizing, including pain in the lower abdomen and groin, and sometimes in the legs and lower back; there is a frequent desire to pass urine, and this can be painful and accompanied by a burning sensation. Sometimes traces of blood are present in the urine.

There has never been any evidence to show that osteopathic lesions cause true cystitis. However, as I explained in Chapter Three, osteopathic lesions can sometimes mimic the effects of other complaints, and spinal lesions found in the upper lumbar and pelvic regions can *mimic* symptoms similar to those of cystitis. This pseudo-cystitis also seems to occur most frequently in women, who complain of pain in the lower abdomen and groin, down the inner thighs and lower back, with a frequent desire to pass urine. With this complaint, however, there are no signs of blood and no burning sensation, factors which are very important in the differential diagnosis: if any blood is noticed in the urine the osteopath will immediately refer the patient back to her doctor.

It is in cases where no bacterial infection or other pathology is found that osteopathic lesions are frequently found, particularly of the upper lumbar spine and the pubic symphysis joint at the front of the pelvis. This joint is vulnerable to strains and the lesion is found more often in women than men, probably due to the stresses and strains placed upon it by childbirth. When the osteopath finds and corrects the problem the symptoms of 'cystitis' will very often subside.

This lesion may also be associated with weakness and imbalances of the abdominal and thigh muscles. This makes it necessary for the osteopath to examine and correct faulty mobility and alignment of the upper lumbar joints, as this area is the source for the distribution of nerves to the thighs and abdomen, and imbalances in these muscles can cause recurrent lesions of the pubic symphysis joint.

The Menopause

The menopause, commonly known as 'the change of life', is a perfectly natural process which many women go through with no problems other than mild symptoms of hot flushes and increased perspiration. However, there are others for whom this time of life can be very distressing. They may suffer symptoms of nervousness, fatigue, depression, irritability, insomnia, palpitations, menstrual disturbances, numbness and tingling in the arms, legs and elsewhere, digestive disorders, urinary increase and incontinence, and back-pain.

As a rule, it is only the back-pain that will prompt a woman to visit an osteopath; most women would not think of doing so for other menopausal symptoms. It is during the consultation that many of the symptoms of the menopause become recognizable to the osteopath, and he needs to be careful to distinguish whether the back-pain has been caused by some strain or injury, or whether it is due to a condition known as osteoporosis.

Osteoporosis is a condition that softens the bones, and can be associated with a deficiency of the hormone oestrogen, whose production decreases during the menopause. I strongly advise women to start taking supplements, particularly calcium and Vitamin D, as early as possible in the menopausal phase, which may help to counteract the softening of the bones. Ideally, women should start to pay serious attention to increase their dietary intake of calcium and Vitamin D when they are nearing the age of forty, in preparation for the menopause, which usually ocurs between the ages of forty and fifty.

When women consult an osteopath for something entirely separate from their menopausal symptoms, they are often surprised and delighted to find that these can be helped, too. It is especially important that any spinal lesions in the upper neck are corrected: lesions in this area, with associated muscular tension, can contribute to and increase the incidence of hot flushes and sweating, as they interfere with circulation in the hypothalamus, the part of the brain that regulates these functions.

For nervousness and insomnia, doctors often prescribe tranquillizers. I feel that these should be treated with some caution; an excessive intake of tranquillizers can deplete the body of essential vitamins and minerals, and even taken for only three or four months they can lead to serious problems of addiction. Rather than relying on chemicals, I prefer to recommend to my women patients that they perform the relaxation exercises described in Chapter Six. In combination with these exercises, some caring advice and a listening ear can render the need for tranquillizers unnecessary, and of course many women find that osteopathic treatment in itself is very relaxing.

Personally, I have found that whatever the menopausal woman is being treated for, the duration of the treatment must be kept short, and the approach should be especially gentle. In my experience, over-prolonged sessions, or manipulative techniques involving the high-speed thrusts which produce audible 'clicks', can produce unwanted reactions. Most osteopaths are of this opinion, and will take this into consideration when treating women going through the change of life.

Shopping and Your Back

Osteopaths are often told by their women patients that carrying shopping bags gives them back-ache or makes a back-pain worse. The two most common areas of strain are firstly the base of the lower back and secondly in the neck and across the top of the shoulders. What can be done about this problem?

In the UK, most people carry their shopping in bags with handles. In the USA, however, people usually carry handle-less shopping bags clutched close to the body. Most authorities on spinal disorders and back-pain agree that carrying any heavy load is more acceptable to the spine if it is held close to the body. A British osteopath, A. K. Burton, DO, MRO, has researched this theory and has made a comparison between the British and American methods of carrying bags. He reported the results in a paper entitled 'Spinal Strain from Shopping Bags With and Without Handles' (1986).

He took twelve subjects, six males and six females, with no significant history of previous back-pain. Electromyography was used to measure and record the activities of certain groups of back muscles: electrode pads were placed on two areas of the spine, across the top of the shoulders and in the lower back. Each subject was given a bag filled with the amount of groceries that might be carried regularly by a housewife. The subjects then walked on a treadmill for some distance, each carrying both types of shopping bag in turn, while their muscular activity was amplified by the electromyograph and recorded on a computer.

The readings obtained from this experiment showed that the American style of carrying proved to be less of a strain to the spinal muscles than the British way; this was particularly evident in the muscle groups across the top of the shoulders.

Osteopathy for Children

Children who complain of back-pain should never be ignored; back-ache is not a purely adult complaint. And, as we have seen, back problems are becoming alarmingly prevalent in our society.

The ideal medicine is preventative medicine, and it is with children that the prevention of spinal and musculoskeletal problems can really take place. It has been said that our spinal patterns are well developed by the age of ten, by which time many injuries and strains may already have been introduced into the spinal column, laying a foundation for future problems to arise. Prevention therefore needs to start at an early age, by educating children as to how to stand, sit, walk and lift, and how best to look after their spines during daily activities.

There are two ways in which this could be done. Firstly, a programme could be taken in schools at the infant stage, from five to seven years. Even one hour's instruction a week would be of enormous benefit. The sessions could be made into fun periods, but nevertheless instilling the basic principles of good posture. Secondly, it would be excellent if children were to have regular check-ups of their posture and spines. Again, this should be instigated early, for the spine can encounter strain and injury from the time children learn to stand.

In both preventative programmes, osteopaths could play a very important role. They could draw up an educational plan on these lines for their local education authorities, and perhaps attend schools for one or two hours a week to help carry it out. At first glance this might appear to involve the government in additional expense; however, if the incidence of back problems could be reduced the result would be an enormous saving long-term to the National Health Service. For this to happen, osteopaths need to be given an authoritative standing in the community.

Meanwhile, the provision of preventative spinal care for children remains a problem. Osteopaths themselves could offer a better service, for example by putting aside a few hours a week to operate special children's preventative clinics at reduced fees. Some osteopathic associations do run children's clinics, but these are few and far between; there are only two that I know of. One is at the British School of Osteopathy and the other at the British College of Naturopathy and Osteopathy. The London School of Osteopathy is currently trying to organize a similar venture.

Spinal Problems in Children

The two most vulnerable areas of the spine in young children are the neck and the lower back. Osteopathic lesions are often found in the neck area; this is not surprising: one probable reason is that the muscles and bones of the neck have to support the heavy weight of the head. Young babies are particularly prone to suffering from 'jolts' in the neck, at the stage when the muscles are not yet strong enough to support the head.

Young children are just as vulnerable to injuries and strains as adults, particularly nowadays when there is an emphasis on sporting activities and competitive sports both in and out of school; in fact an increasing number of children are sustaining back injuries.

When dealing with children's spinal problems, the osteopath has to be very certain that the complaint has been caused by some injury such as a jolt, wrench or twisting strain. If this cannot be ascertained, it may be advisable for the child to be X-rayed to make sure there is no more serious problem present. For example, as we have already seen, an acute torticollis (wry-neck) which appears for no apparent reason may be the first sign of rheumatoid arthritis, for which any form of manipulation would be definitely contra-indicated.

It is also of paramount importance that the osteopath knows when to call upon or refer a child patient to other specialists. Just recently, for example, a mother brought in her daughter of thirteen who had been complaining for three months of pain in her lower back which she could find no reason for. There was no history of injury or strain, but there was evidence of curvature in her lower back as well as a large patch of hair in this region: all these factors made me decide to send her for X-rays. A patch of hair growing on the back, particularly very low down, can indicate that there is a congenital anomaly present.

The X-ray confirmed my suspicions with a report of spina bifida occulta from the third lumbar vertebra to the first sacral segment inclusive. This is not as serious a condition as the other and probably better-known form of spina bifida, spina bifida vera. Spina bifida occulta is a condition in which one or more vertebrae have not completely formed, and have failed to join up in the mid-line. This defect is present from birth, though it may not be obvious, and can cause many developmental problems. In some cases it causes no pain or, according to some authorities, any other symptoms either. However, others believe that it can give rise to symptoms ranging from mild to severe back-ache, with a high incidence starting around the ages of twelve to fourteen.

In the case of this girl, I referred her to her doctor to seek the opinion of an orthopaedic surgeon. This is not always necessary with this condition; if only one spinal segment is involved, although manipulative thrusts should not be used, osteopathic treatment to the soft tissues and gentle stretching techniques can nearly always eliminate the pain. But this case was more complicated, since there were several segments involved, making the spine vulnerable and weak in this area. This is something this patient will have to bear in mind if she wants to have children in later life, which as we have seen can be a strain on the lower back.

Another common cause of back-ache in children which requires a differential diagnosis is Scheuermann's disease, or juvenile kyphosis. This can also be confirmed by X-ray, where it shows up as an unequal growth of the vertebrae, usually in the thoracic-lumbar region – the middle to lower part of the back in line with the bottom of the rib cage. It appears to be caused by trauma, infection or nutritional deficiencies. Although osteopathic treatment cannot cure this condition, it can help to relieve muscular tensions and improve circulation to the area and also prevent the spine from becoming strained above and below the affected area.

It is important for parents to take children's complaints of pain seriously: not only could back-pain indicate a serious condition, but also, as I have already stressed, treatment in childhood could prevent many problems developing in later life.

CASE HISTORY (I)
Danny, a very active six-year-old, was brought in to see me by his mother. That afternoon he had been playing on the climbing apparatus in a playground and had fallen off, landing on top of

his head. An X-ray at the local casualty department showed nothing abnormal, but since falling he had had a pain in his neck when he turned his head to the left.

Examination of Danny found no obvious postural imbalances or spinal curvatures, but I found some very tender spots in the upper to mid neck region, and movement in this area of his neck was restricted. Even quite young children generally enjoy treatment, incidentally, so long as they are given very gentle techniques which do not startle them. I treated Danny in this way, with some very gentle osteopathic manipulation, and normal movement was immediately restored, though he still felt some discomfort when turning his head to the left. I made another appointment for him in two days' time. On this visit he said that the pain had completely gone, and he could move his neck with complete freedom.

CASE HISTORY (2)

Irene was a twelve-year-old, very tall for her age; she had been complaining of low-back pain for several weeks, although there was no definite history of injury or strain to account for it. On examination, her lumbosacral (lower back) region was painful to mild, springing pressure. Because of her height she was inclined to slouch, but there were no obvious developmental or structural curvatures. Because nothing specific had started the pain, and there were no obvious osteopathic lesions present, I decided to have her X-rayed.

The X-ray showed a spina bifida occulta of the first sacral segment. I treated her by applying very gentle osteopathic treatment, and after several weeks her back pain disappeared. During this period I gave her advice on posture and how to lift correctly, by moving the leg muscles rather than her back muscles. I gave her exercises to strengthen the lower muscles of her back, and encouraged her to go swimming. Once the back-pain had gone, I encouraged her to attend every three months for a spinal check-up. She did this for a couple of years until she moved away from the district, and during this time she remained completely free of pain.

Swimming, by the way, is an excellent exercise for the back, with the exception of the butterfly stroke and diving, either of which can further damage problem backs.

CASE HISTORY (3)

As I mentioned in an earlier chapter, neck problems in children often seem to be brought on by stress. For example, a boy of fifteen was brought to me by his father suffering an acute torticollis. He told me that the day before he had simply turned his head, which had left him with an ache in the neck. The next morning when he woke his head was pulled to one side, and any movement away from the side of the spasm caused excruciating pain. His general health was satisfactory, with no recent history of any ear, nose or throat infections, injuries or accidents. When I talked with him, however, I found that he was concerned about his forthcoming exams, and I felt that he was under some emotional strain and stress, and that this could have been a contributory factor. I believe that children under stress may be tense when they sleep, and tossing and turning in bed can cause the neck to turn awkwardly, bringing on this kind of problem.

Treatment consisted of very gentle inhibitory pressure to the involved muscles, as well as correction of a sacral dysfunction and a spinal thoracic lesion between the shoulder blades. There was an osteopathic lesion in his upper neck which I treated using the non-traumatic approach of functional-type diagnosis and treatment, since it would have been unwise to have used a thrust-type manipulation at this stage.

During the whole treatment regime, I discussed his examination ordeal with him; he seemed to have no belief in his own abilities, and I tried to reassure him and boost his confidence. After the treatment, he felt easier, and the neck was easier to move. However, his neck and head were still not totally straight, and he was still in some pain.

On re-examination I could still detect the lesion in the upper neck, but the muscle guarding around the joint was considerably reduced. I gave this area some further treatment, this time using a muscular-energy-type manipulation. This non-traumatic technique was carried out by taking the boy's neck and head to the point of localized restriction of the joint and then asking him to turn his head in the other direction while applying counter-force for several seconds. After repeating this three or four times, the lesion was reduced, the boy could move his neck fully, and his head and neck were once more sitting straight.

I saw him a couple of days later for re-evaluation. He was perfectly well and free of pain, and I could no longer find any osteopathic lesion in the upper neck. Of course, osteopathy alone could not cure his anxieties, but I hope that the relaxing physical treatment combined with my reassurance may have helped him in this respect.

In addition to the conventional manipulative techniques, there is another extremely gentle technique from which children and even babies can benefit. This is cranial osteopathy, which will be described in the next chapter.

CHAPTER TWELVE

CRANIAL OSTEOPATHY:

THE EXPANSION OF A CONCEPT

Gently manipulating the cranium, the skull, is really an expansion of the concepts and principles of Dr Andrew Taylor Still, and cranial osteopathy is still a developing art. The technique was founded some fifty years ago by an American osteopath, Dr William Garner Sutherland, who outlined its principles in the 1930s, calling it 'Craniosacral Therapy'.

He based his treatment on what he called the 'primary respiratory mechanism', a natural rhythmical movement within the central nervous system, in which an important part is played by the mobility of the skull bones, the sacrum and coccyx (the tail bone). Although his theories have yet to be scientifically proven, the excellent clinical results achieved so far in many conditions make the subject worthy of continued research in order to achieve wider acceptance.

If you look at a skull you can see that it is not solid bone, but is made up of a number of sections. By touching the skull very lightly, Sutherland discovered – contrary to the medical and anatomical opinion of his time – that these sections actually move. Moreover, he noticed that they move with a distinct pattern, regularly expanding and contracting in a pulse-like rhythm. It is believed that this cyclical rhythm is influenced by and influences the circulation of the cerebrospinal fluid, and cranial osteopaths call it the 'cranial rhythmic impulse'.

Osteopaths are trained to develop a very fine tactile perception of subtle movements in the human musculoskeletal system, and cranial osteopaths are trained to measure the cranial rhythmic impulse. By laying his hands gently and lightly on the skull, so that the contact is barely perceptible to the patient, the cranial osteopath can feel this subtle rhythmical expansion and contraction of the skull.

The average rate of the cranial rhythmic impulse in a healthy person is ten to fourteen per minute; it can be a little higher in children. However, the presence of physical trauma (minor or major), psychological stress, or diseases (particularly infections) can affect the rate of the impulse. So can exercise, deep breathing and osteopathic cranio-sacral treatment.

Not all osteopaths practise or even believe in the cranial osteopathic concepts. This may be due to scepticism, a lack of knowledge and understanding, or an inability to feel and detect the very tiny movement in the skull bones and membranes. I believe that any osteopath who will take the time and trouble to develop the necessary sensitivity of touch should be able to experience the subtle movements of the skull. Once he has achieved this, his doubts about the cranial concepts will be dispelled – especially once he becomes proficient enough to use it in his treatment regime and witness its results for himself. For this technique can achieve some remarkable results in conditions that do not respond to the usual osteopathic techniques, or the other forms of complementary or orthodox medicine.

Cranial osteopathy has been found to be useful and effective in such conditions as migraine, trigeminal neuralgia, tic douloureux, Bell's palsy, eye, ear and nose problems, allergies, asthma, anxiety, depression, learning and behavioural difficulties in children, headaches, and even conditions such as low-back pain, sciatica and degenerative arthritic conditions. Many of these are conditions which osteopaths found it particularly difficult to treat until the cranial osteopathic concepts and treatment were established.

One reason for its ability to promote healing in so many conditions lies in the fact that very gently compressing the skull seems to stimulate the flow of the cerebrospinal fluid which circulates around the brain and through the spinal cord. This fluid is believed to carry pituitary hormones, enzymes, and antibodies which are essential for the health of the body's cells. Although its action and effects have not been fully scientifically assessed, extensive research is currently going on within the osteopathic profession into what controls the circulation of the cerebrospinal fluid, and its effects.

Cranial Lesions

The normal adult skull is made up of twenty-two bones. Lesions can occur in the sutures, or joints, between these as in other joints, and these can cause local and distant symptoms in the function of the body via the communicative and fluid systems,

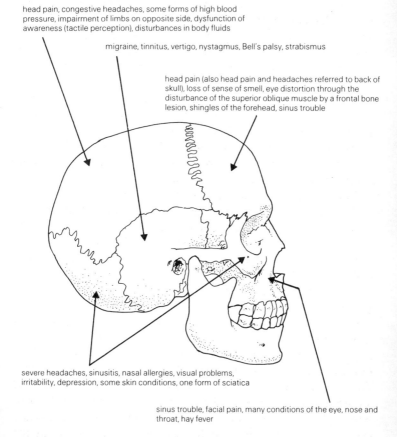

head pain, congestive headaches, some forms of high blood pressure, impairment of limbs on opposite side, dysfunction of awareness (tactile perception), disturbances in body fluids

migraine, tinnitus, vertigo, nystagmus, Bell's palsy, strabismus

head pain (also head pain and headaches referred to back of skull), loss of sense of smell, eye distortion through the disturbance of the superior oblique muscle by a frontal bone lesion, shingles of the forehead, sinus trouble

severe headaches, sinusitis, nasal allergies, visual problems, irritability, depression, some skin conditions, one form of sciatica

sinus trouble, facial pain, many conditions of the eye, nose and throat, hay fever

Figure 19. Cranial bone lesions and some of their possible effects.

the cerebrospinal fluid and the circulation. Probably most important of all, cranial lesions can and do disturb the regular flow of the cerebrospinal fluid.

When treating the cranio-sacral system, the osteopath recognizes a total of 117 possible basic lesions, which stem from a variety of causes. The very first stress that the human head can encounter is during the birth process; the descent of the foetus through the birth canal can often lead to distortions of the skull. Many of these spontaneously correct themselves during the first few days after birth. However, in some cases they do not, and this can lead to a number of health problems. Blows or bumps on the head can obviously produce cranial lesions; they do not have to be particularly severe to disturb the movement of the cranial bones. Whiplash injuries are another common cause of disturbance in the cranial mechanism; it can also be disrupted by dental surgery, especially difficult operations involving tooth extraction.

The osteopath notes cranial dysfunctions by observing the symmetry of the head and facial bones. Distortions may be seen in the forehead, which, when viewed from above, may appear to have moved slightly sideways. Any asymmetry may indicate some kind of cranial fault, such as one bulging eye, a deeper fold from the nose down to one corner of the mouth, a widening or narrowing of the orbits (the bony cavities which contain the eyeballs), one ear sticking out more than the other, or a larger nasal opening on one side than the other.

Cranial Treatment

Treatment of a cranial lesion is performed with the utmost gentleness. The osteopath usually starts by standing behind the patient and cupping their head in the palms of his hands. When he senses the tension and restriction that indicates the presence of a lesion, he will treat the area by moulding it into a more correct position and improving the mobility of the joint.

One widely used cranial technique is a gentle compression of the base of the skull. It has been said that no one is too ill to receive this form of treatment, and it can affect a multitude of conditions, which is obviously extremely helpful. Clinically, this particular technique has proved to be successful in lowering fevers, hastening and promoting the healing of fractures, and boosting the immune system by stimulating the activity of the spleen. It helps the body to absorb calcium and other deposits associated with degenerative arthritic complaints. It can also, in some cases, reduce tissue engorgement and swelling.

Sometimes the osteopath may need to insert his thumbs or fingers inside the patient's mouth in order to correct cranial lesions and lesions of the palate. This may sound unpleasant , but it rarely is – and, I hasten to add, disposable finger cots are always used for the sake of hygiene. One reason for performing this technique is to correct lesions of the jaw joint known as the temporo-mandibular joint, which are quite common. With his fingers inside the mouth, the osteopath will *gently* move the jaw bones in all directions, to mobilize the mandible, the jaw bone, so as to free any restriction that may exist.

To emphasize just how gentle cranial treatment should be, the late Dr Dennis Brookes, who was president of the Natural Therapeutic and Osteopathic Society and probably the foremost authority on cranial osteopathy in Europe, used repeatedly to remind osteopaths that while treating the skull they should imagine that they were holding a little bird between their hands. A good indication that the osteopath's pressure has been at the right level is when the patient who has just received treatment remarks how relaxed he or she feels.

In fact the observer of a cranial osteopathic session, and even the patient, may get the impression that the osteopath is doing no more than laying his hands on the patient's head. This is because the techniques are extremely subtle, involving microscopic movements. When I myself am performing cranial treatment I tell my receptionist I must not be disturbed by anything or anyone; this is to ensure that I can give my total concentration to the therapy in an unhurried and relaxed atmosphere. It is also important that the osteopath does not suddenly remove his hands from the patient's head during a cranial motion correction.

Let us look at some of the conditions that cranial osteopathy can help.

Migraine

This form of recurrent intense headache is a very common condition. These headaches can be throbbing, boring or pounding, and can be truly agonizing; they are usually preceded by visual disturbances such as flashing lights or blurred vision, and there is often a feeling of nausea; many migraine sufferers have attacks of vomiting. People who suffer from severe migraines usually need to go to bed in a quiet, darkened room during an attack.

One patient of mine, a man in his sixties, would need to get away from it all and lie down quietly as soon as he experienced visual disturbances in the form of bright lights. If these started up when he was out shopping with his wife, he could abort a bad migraine by going back to his car and lying down. But if he was unable to do this, he would usually get a severe headache which kept him in bed for at least twenty-four hours.

Migraine patients are often the sort of people who pursue life to the full; they tend to be compulsive, eager-beaver types, who lie awake at night because they can't switch themselves off. Migraine attacks can be triggered by a variety of factors, including worry, depression, mental or physical over-exertion, over-excitement, noise, certain foods, changes in atmospheric conditions, bright lights, prolonged watching of television, films or VDUs, alcohol, irregular mealtimes, menstruation and the premenstrual period – and this list could go on!

However, the precise *cause* of migraine headaches is not known. The general opinion is that they start with a constriction of the blood vessels in the brain, followed by an expansion of these blood vessels, which is then followed by a build-up of cerebral fluid. The resultant pressure is thought to be responsible for the excruciating head pain.

Orthodox medical treatment usually consists of certain drugs. If the migraines are known to be triggered by an allergic response, the patient will have to avoid the foods concerned.

Osteopathic manipulative treatment can be very successful with migraine in many – though not all – cases. Some cases can be completely cured; in others, treatment will increase the length of time between attacks; but on some occasions, unfortunately, it will have no beneficial results.

On examining a migraine sufferer, the osteopath often finds that the upper neck muscles are very tense and rigid, with the three upper vertebrae restricted in the normal movement; his fingers will feel this as a sense of wooden stiffness. There may also be restriction and tenderness at the upper thoracic and rib areas; and the area between the shoulder blades – the sixth to ninth thoracic vertebrae – may also be tender, with tension and restriction.

It has been said of migraine that if the cranial osteopath can obtain a release of the temporal bone in the skull, he will completely cure the migraine, and this has indeed been shown to be so over the years. However, the correction is not an easy one to make, and it may take some time to accomplish. So both the osteopath and the patient may need some perseverance!

CASE HISTORY

A woman of forty-two was recommended to consult me by one of my osteopathic colleagues. She had suffered from frequent migraines since childhood and during an attack would experience a great deal of pain and tension in the neck, while her vision would become blurred in one eye.

Before consulting me she had tried taking a herbal remedy, which can be quite successful in some cases of migraine; in her case, however, it was ineffective. When I examined her, I found lesions in the neck causing tenderness, tension and restriction; I also found a lesion in the pelvis. Probably most important of all, however, I found cranial bone dysfunction. On her fourth visit she told me that she had not had a migraine for the whole month since her previous treatment and was feeling better than she had done for years. She has been completely clear of migraine for some time now, and I have discharged her.

Tinnitus

This condition is characterized by a frequent and irritating noise in the inner ear; it can be similar to the roaring of the sea, like the sound you can hear if you hold a conch shell against your ear. It can also be experienced as buzzing, whistling, roaring or hissing, and it can be either intermittent or, worse still, continuous. It is extremely distressing, and many sufferers understandably become very depressed. The only way some of them can get to sleep is by playing background music to drown out the sound.

Tinnitus may have a number of causes, and the mechanism by which it is produced is still obscure. Its symptoms may be associated with a number of ear disorders, and also with heart disease, hardening of the arteries, high blood pressure, traumas to the head, and very loud noises which can affect the hearing (such as working with a road drill).

From the cranial viewpoint, tinnitus can be caused by a disturbance in the flow of blood due to a temporal bone lesion. The temporal bone has been called the 'troublemaker' in the head, and it is often disturbed in tinnitus, migraine, Bell's palsy, trigeminal neuralgia and other conditions. Provided the blood vessels involved have not progressed too far with sclerotic changes – which would mean that they have become defective from a hardening process – correcting and releasing the cranial mechanism has in some cases given total relief of symptoms.

Bell's Palsy

This is a condition that produces a paralysis of the facial muscles, usually on one side. It can be caused by infections (including some of a respiratory nature), colds, or sitting with one side of the face exposed to a severe draught: for example, when the window of the driver's seat is open in a moving car, and the draught blows through to the back of the car, rebounding on to the front passenger's side at face level. Another common cause is trauma, such as dental extraction, which can sometimes strain the cranial mechanism, or trauma to the neck region creating osteopathic lesions of the cervical spine.

Bell's palsy can appear very suddenly, and can be rather alarming. The paralysed face muscles give the face a distorted look; in bad cases the mouth normally droops to one side, causing speech impediment, and the eye on that side is unable to close, which makes it vulnerable to foreign particles like dust and flies. Fortunately, for some patients, a spontaneous recovery can sometimes happen within a couple of weeks. However, if this does not happen, cranial osteopathic treatment can often be very beneficial, especially in those cases caused by trauma.

Trigeminal Neuralgia

This is a fairly common condition that causes intense pain in the face due to irritation of the trigeminal nerve, which is also known as the fifth cranial nerve and is the largest of the twelve cranial nerves, covering a wide area. The pain can be experienced around the forehead, nose and mouth, as the nerve has three divisions supplying these areas. In severe cases the sufferer may have a spasmodic facial twitch which, like the pain, can be triggered by minor stimulative actions like washing the face, eating and drinking, sitting in a cool draught, and even by talking.

Conventional medical treatment for trigeminal neuralgia consists of prescribing drugs for sedation and pain relief, operating to section off the affected branch of the nerve, or injecting alcohol or other substances to block the nerve pathway.

Osteopaths are of the opinion that this very painful condition is often caused by trauma to the head or jaw bone, and in many instances they find a restriction of two specific bones within the skull, which places considerable tension on the membranes, which in turn disturbs the trigeminal nerve. There may well also be lesions in the neck. It is important however to make a differential diagnosis, since trigeminal neuralgic pain may have other causes, such as infection of the teeth and nasal sinus passages, or herpes, as well as other more serious causes.

Cranial osteopathic treatment will be aimed at releasing the cranial restriction, particularly at the temporal bone, which is often found to be asymmetrical and lesioned. The osteopath will also make a careful examination of the patient's jaw joint and will note any tenderness or tension in the facial muscles. To detect whether the jaw alignment is incorrect, with one side restricted in its movements, he will lightly place his fingers over the joints and ask the patient to open his mouth slowly. If there is a problem within the joint of the jaw, the osteopath will note that the chin will deviate to one side, and instead of a smooth gliding action he will feel an irregular movement.

To obtain relief of trigeminal neuralgia, it is usually necessary to balance the jaw joint. This can generally be done by osteopathic manipulative techniques, though should these fail the patient is best referred to a dental surgeon. As well as cranial manipulation, the osteopath will probably also give particular attention to the joints in the upper neck; manipulating this area has been known to achieve very good results with this disturbing ailment.

Eye Problems

Cranial osteopathy has proved to be very successful with certain eye problems, particularly conditions such as strabismus (squint) and nystagmus (involuntary jerky movements of the eyes), which can be helped by the osteopath releasing tensions in the membranes of the skull.

The eyes rely on an exchange of arterial, venous and lymphatic fluids for their normal function. There are primarily three systems of blood supply to the eye and four drainage systems; their correct and uninterrupted flow is vital to the health of the eye. Membranous tensions of the skull, and also abnormal tensions of the muscles involved in eye movement, can impede this normal flow.

Osteopaths, more so in America than in the UK, use a variety of approaches that may help in the management of some eye problems. Manipulative techniques to the neck and upper thoracic spinal areas can be of importance. Treating the Chapman's reflex points can also sometimes be helpful. And so can cranial manipulative techniques, including specific gentle manipulation to the eye muscles themselves. Osteopaths, particularly in America, have reported favourable management of such problems as conjunctivitis, iritis, retinitis and choroiditis, which are all inflammatory conditions of the eyes. Even glaucoma has been helped by osteopathic management, presumably by decreasing the intra-ocular tension, the internal tension and pressure of the eyeball.

I would never suggest that osteopaths are eye specialists; in most cases people presenting with eye problems like those described above have already had a medical/opthalmological diagnosis. Osteopaths are willing to try to help them, preferably in conjunction with the opthalmic specialist. They will make their own diagnosis of the cranial and spinal lesions involved; recognizing and treating these can often be very helpful, alongside orthodox medical treatment.

Sinusitis

Acute sinusitis, that is sinusitis that is recent and only short-term, is usually caused by respiratory tract infections, such as colds and influenza. Symptoms include facial pain, pain in and around the eyes, and headaches, particularly in the frontal part of the head. The patient may also suffer from a nasal discharge, blocked nose and possibly a high temperature. These symptoms usually clear up once the infection has been controlled.

Chronic or recurrent sinusitis may be associated with nasal allergies and cranial lesions, both of which can be helped, and on many occasions completely alleviated by a combination of general osteopathic manipulation and the cranial osteopathic approach. This works by assisting venous and lymphatic drainage from the head and neck, which helps to relieve the congestion in the head, giving nature's resistive forces a better chance to combat and clear up any infection.

In addition, the osteopath will give attention to and correct upper thoracic and cervical lesions, and will make sure that the collar bones and ribs are moving freely, without restriction. Finally, he will give treatment to the cranium, including the facial bones. I cannot recall a single sinusitis patient treated in this way who has not felt immediate relief of the pain and of the clogged, congested sensation in the air passages of the nose.

Self-help for Sinusitis. The sufferer can also be taught to give self-manipulative pressure when in need and unable to reach an osteopath. It is very simple to do. Place your elbows on a table, put one thumb on top of the other and place these inside the roof of your mouth at the back. Let the natural weight of your head rest on your thumbs for five to ten minutes. This helps to promote better lymphatic and venous drainage from the head.

Another useful self-help method is to circle the forefingers around the prominences of your cheekbones, and pull the bones sideways, holding for a minute or so. This helps to free the nasal openings, clearing the air passage through the nose.

Steam inhalants can also give relief. Fill a basin with boiling water, and then sit over the basin with a towel over your head, and inhale the steam for five to ten minutes. This helps to de-congest the head and also helps the infected sinus passages.

Skin Problems and Allergies

Healthy skin relies, amongst other things, on a normal blood supply. Osteopathic treatment to correct the nerve and blood supply to the affected area can on occasions help. Many allergies and skin problems have been known to respond to cranial osteopathy, by means of its balancing effects on the hormonal system and body chemistry.

CASE HISTORY

I recently treated a woman of forty-three who was suffering from chronic urticaria angioedema: this is an allergic type of skin eruption which appears as red weals on the skin, often with swollen eyelids, feet, hands and mucous membranes. In this particular case the skin reaction was always worse around three to four o'clock in the afternoon, with particular swelling of the face and lips. When this lady consulted me she had been suffering with these distressing symptoms for just over eleven months.

A local doctor had carried out allergy tests, showing that she was reactive to wheat and soya and extremely reactive to aspirin. However, eliminating these from her diet did not help. In addi-tion, her general health was not very good; she had periods of depression, felt tired and generally run down, and suffered at least one migraine a week.

During the routine consultation she told me that her symptoms were definitely aggravated by emotional stress. Blood tests taken at her local hospital had revealed nothing abnormal, and medically prescribed antihistamine had not helped. She had been told that corticosteroids might stop the reaction, but since she might have to take them for an indefinite period she refused this form of treatment. She had also visited a private allergy clinic and an acupuncturist, to no avail.

There are several associated causes of urticaria and angioedema, including allergies to certain drugs and injections, insect stings and bites, reactions to particular foods and even as an aftermath of certain viral infections. Although these are the more common and best-known causes, other urticaria reactions are of unknown origins. Bearing this in mind, and since she had not responded to anything else, I decided to give osteopathy and cranio-sacral therapy a try.

When I examined her I found lesions in the lumbar, mid-thoracic and upper cervical spine, and I also detected definite cranial bone restriction in the skull. I treated her weekly, using manipulation to release all these tensions and restrictions. On the first treatment only the spinal lesions were treated, which made no difference at all to her symptoms. On her second visit I gave her cranial osteopathy. Following this she reported that she had had a bad skin reaction for one day after the treatment, but for the next three days was much better. After the fifth treatment she was very much better and had no problems for several days. Considering that she had suffered the red weals on her skin every day for eleven months, both she and I were delighted.

At the time of writing, she has now been totally symptom-free for several months. When I discussed this case with a colleague, he suggested that the improvement might have been caused by a placebo effect: that is, that being treated with care and concern might have been enough to achieve the positive result. I don't accept this, however: this woman had already consulted several practitioners who I am sure were equally caring.

Cranial Osteopathy for Babies and Children

Treating babies and young children with cranial osteopathy can at times have very significant therapeutic results. Conditions for which it is particularly indicated in children are learning and behavioural disorders, including abnormal fears, hyperactivity, dyslexia, and the more serious conditions of cerebral palsy and autism.

Some American cranial osteopaths have found that hyperactive children, and children suffering from abnormal fears or lack of ability to concentrate, very often suffer from a particular cranial bone lesion. Once this has been corrected the child's behavioural problems have improved dramatically, usually over a short period of time. Sometimes an immediate response is obtained; some hyperactive children have been known to fall asleep on the treatment couch!

Cerebral palsy is the term used for damage sustained to the central nervous system, resulting in spasticity, lack of coordination and involuntary movements. Osteopaths using cranial techniques, involving very gentle and highly skilled cranial manipulation, have reported sufficient improvement in spasticity in such cases to make this treatment very worthwhile.

Obviously, when treating children the osteopath will avoid using heavy or harsh techniques that might hurt the child and lose its confidence, making further treatment difficult or impossible. As I hope I have made clear, cranial osteopathy is performed with the utmost gentleness, no matter what age the patient is.

As I mentioned above, cranial osteopathy is always carried out in a relaxed atmosphere. Let me tell you about a mother who brings her daughter in for osteopathic and cranial therapy. Each time the session reaches the point where I perform the cranial therapy on the child's head, the mother falls asleep – she tells me that this is because simply watching the treatment relaxes her so much!

Treating Other Areas of the Body

Let me finish by citing two case histories showing how effective cranial osteopathy can be in treating areas other than the skull.

CASE HISTORY (1)

A woman of fifty-six fell heavily on her right buttock while walking in the snow. She came to see me three days after the accident, limping because of the pain. I found that there was some heavy bruising on the area where she had fallen, and it was so painful that she could not tolerate me touching her there.

During the examination I checked the function and structural alignment of her pelvic bones, as sometimes a heavy fall like this on one buttock can disturb the structural relationship of the pelvic bone to the sacrum, but I found no such problem. As the area was so painful my choice of treatment was limited. I therefore decided to give some compression to the skull to encourage the flow of the cerebrospinal fluid; this can at times help with pain and with healing injured tissues. I used this compression for about five minutes, and stopped when the patient reported that she was feeling a little warmth around the right sacro-iliac area and buttock. To my delight when she stood up she reported that the pain was less, and she was able to walk without the limp. Next day I contacted her to ask whether the improvements had remained, and she answered: 'Most definitely.'

I was very pleased with this quick recovery, particularly because if limping is prolonged, it can lead to other mechanical problems.

CASE HISTORY (2)

A man of twenty-seven fell from a scaffolding rig, landing heavily on the right side of his shoulder and head. He did not lose consciousness at the time, but as there was marked swelling and bruising over the right parietal bone at the side of the skull, his friends insisted on taking him to hospital. Here X-rays were taken, which showed that there were no fractures in either the skull or shoulder.

He consulted me the same night to see whether I could do anything about his shoulder which was very painful and stiff – so much so that he could not tolerate any pressure or soft-tissue manipulation on it. I decided to use gentle compression techniques around the occipital area at the base of the skull, and treated him in this way for ten minutes. When I had finished, he remarked how much easier the pain felt in his shoulder, and I could see a visible reduction in the swelling on the right side of his skull. Easing the pain allowed me to apply gentle mobilizing techniques to his shoulder, where there was already an obvious improvement in mobility.

After an injury like this one would expect the patient's shoulder to be very stiff the following day; however, my patient reported that he had hardly any stiffness at all.

Finally, here is the personal view of Mrs F. B., aged seventy-six, after receiving this form of treatment.

'Having received a great deal of practical help for osteoarthritis which frees me from pain and keeps the elderly limbs moving far more freely than I could ever have hoped for, I now have further cause for gratitude in the experience of cranial osteopathy.

'Without any previous explanation, Mr Masters placed his hands under my head from behind as I lay on the couch. It felt as though he was hooking his fingers under the edge of my skull, lifting gently, then pressing and holding the position for some while.

'I was wondering vaguely what this was all about, being unable to imagine how it was helping the bits of me that were currently painful. Then I realized there was a "peaceful" warmth suffusing my neck and back of the head. Slowly there was a shifting of pressure. My head felt light – almost weightless – tensions in limbs and body slowly relaxed, they too became light and weightless. The hands moved over the scalp and fingers pressed firmly on temples and forehead, following some strange pattern.

'Then came a sense of blood stimulation. I remember thinking, "Well, this must be good for my poor circulation. I feel good and rested with a general feeling of well-being."

'After this session Mr Masters explained the basic reasons for this treatment, which were fully justified by my experience, not only on this first occasion but on two subsequent sessions. I must stress here that in case anyone thinks I was subjected in any way to suggestion, I assure them I was told nothing prior to the first treatment and had never heard of cranial osteopathy before. I sincerely hope it becomes part of the great work which helps so many sufferers.'

AFTERWORD

As we have seen, the scope of osteopathy is very wide – much wider than the treatment of back-pain. It does not claim to be a cure-all, and cannot be one hundred per cent effective in every complaint. However, it can achieve remarkable results in a variety of disorders, particularly those of a functional nature where there are no organic or pathological complications. Even in some pathological conditions osteopathy can be of enormous benefit, as we have seen in the case of degenerative arthritic complaints, for example.

Osteopaths today have a very wide selection of techniques to draw on, with the emphasis on a gentle approach, which makes osteopathy a safe and effective form of therapy for all age-groups. Indeed, its beneficial effects, not only with musculoskeletal disorders, but also on general health, are making it increasingly popular with the general public. As a result doctors are becoming more aware of the service and benefits that osteopaths have to offer, and on occasions will recommend their treatment. However, there is still a need for improved cooperation and communication between the two professions, which can only be for the good of patients.

So far, statutory recognition has eluded osteopaths in Britain, partly because the osteopaths themselves have been in disagreement over various aspects of the profession. To solve this problem there needs to be unity within the profession as a whole, so that a nationally recognized standard of education can be established. It is encouraging that positive steps are already being taken towards this goal; I feel sure that osteopaths and the public alike look forward to the day when it has been achieved and osteopathy can gain the authoritative standing in the community which it deserves.

APPENDIX

WHERE TO FIND AN OSTEOPATH

Probably the best method of finding an osteopath is through the recommendation of a friend or relative who has had good osteopathic care and treatment from a practitioner. Failing this, you can contact the various national organizations or schools who hold registers of qualified osteopaths.

BRITAIN

The London School of Osteopathy, registered office: 110 Lower Richmond Road, Putney, London SW15 ILN. Graduates from this school use the initials DO, MNTOS and are members of the Natural Therapeutic and Osteopathic Society.

The British College of Naturopathy and Osteopathy, Frazer House, 6 Netherall Gardens, London NW3 5RR. Graduates from this college use the initials ND and/or DO, MBNOA and are members of the British Naturopathic and Osteopathic Association, registered office: 6 Netherall Gardens, London NW3 5RR.

The British School of Osteopathy, 1–4 Suffolk Street, London SW1 4HG. Graduates from this college (and of the European School of Osteopathy) use the initials MRO and are members of the General Council and Register of Osteopaths, 21 Suffolk Street, London SW1 4HG.

The European School of Osteopathy, 104 Tonbridge Road, Maidstone, Kent ME16 8SL.

Andrew Still College of Osteopathy, The Registrar, 7 Sidewood Road, London SE9 2EZ. Graduates from this college use the initials DO, MBEOA and are members of the British European Osteopathic Association, secretary's address as above.

College of Osteopaths Practitioners' Association, 21 Manor Road North, Wallington, Surrey SM6 7NS. Graduates from this college and members use the initials FCO or MCO.

The London College of Osteopathic Medicine, 8–10 Boston Place, London NWI 6QH. Offers post-graduate training for doctors.

The Institute for Complementary Medicine, 21 Portland Place, London WIN 3AF. The Institute for Complementary Medicine holds a list of qualified practitioners in osteopathy and other natural therapies.

AMERICA

American Osteopathic Association and Canadian Osteopathic Association, PO Bin 1050, Carmel, California 93921, USA.

American Academy of Osteopathy, 2630 Airport Road, Colorado Springs, Colorado 80910, USA.

AUSTRALIA

Australia Osteopathic Association, 71 Collins Street, Victoria, Australia.

NEW ZEALAND

New Zealand Register of Osteopaths, 92 Hurstmere Road, Takapuna, Auckland, New Zealand.

BIBLIOGRAPHY

Arbuckle, Beryl E., n.d. *Selected Writings*, American Academy of Osteopathy, Colorado.

Berkow, Robert (ed.), 1977. *The Merck Manual*, thirteenth edition, Merck, Sharp and Dohme Research, New Jersey.

Bourdillon, J. F., 1973. *Spinal Manipulation*, Heinemann, London.

Bowles, Charles H., 1955-7. 'Functional Orientation for Technique', Parts 1-3, *Year Book of the American Academy of Osteopathy*, Colorado.

Bradbury, Parnell, 1957. *Healing By Hand*, The Harvill Press, London.

Brookes, Denis, 1981. *Lectures on Cranial Osteopathy*, Thorsons Publishers Ltd, Northamptonshire.

Burton, A. K., 1986. 'Spinal Strain from Shopping Bags With and Without Handles', *Applied Ergonomics*, 17/1, pp. 19–25.

Cannon, Alexander, 1939. *Sleeping Through Space*, Walcott Publishing Co., Nottingham.

Cole, George M., 1972. 'Handbook of Osteopathic Guidelines for Student and Physician', *Year Book of the American Academy of Osteopathy*, Colorado.

Critchley, Macdonald (ed.), 1978. *Butterworth's Medical Dictionary*, Butterworth and Co., London.

Cyriax, James, 1949. *Osteopathy and Manipulation*, Crosby, Lockwood and Sons, London.

Downing, Carter Harrison, 1935. *Osteopathic Principles in Disease*, Ricardo J. Orozco, San Francisco, California.

Hartman, Laurie S., 1985. *Handbook of Osteopathic Technique*, Hutchinson and Co., London.

Hoag, J. Marshall, 1970. 'Theoretic Analysis of Osteopathic Lesions', *Year Book of the American Academy of Osteopathy*, Colorado.

Hoag, J. Marshall, Cole, W. V. and Bradford, S. G., 1969. *Osteopathic Medicine*, McGraw-Hill, New York.

Hoover, H. V., 1969. 'Hopeful Road Ahead for Osteopathy', *Year Book of the American Academy of Osteopathy*, Colorado.

Jones, Lawrence H., 1981. *Strain and Counterstrain*, American Academy of Osteopathy, Colorado.

Kappler, Robert E., 1973. 'The Role of Psoas Mechanism in Low-Back Complaints', *Year Book of the American Academy of Osteopathy*, Colorado.

Kirk, Chester E., 1977. 'Biodynamics of Self-Administered Manipulation', *Year Book of the American Academy of Osteopathy*, Colorado.

Koor, Irvin, M., 1979. *Collected Papers*, American Academy of Osteopathy, Colorado.

Lace, Mary V., 1945. *Massage and Medical Gymnastics*, J. and A. Churchill Ltd, London.

Lowry, Gerald, 1935. *Helping Hands*, Bodley Head, London.

Magoun, H. I., 1965. 'Abnormalities in the Sacral Base Plane as an Underlying Factor in Osteopathic Pathology of the Spine', *Year Book of the American Academy of Osteopathy*, Colorado.

——, 1976. 'Whiplash Injury – A Greater Lesion Complex', *Year Book of the American Academy of Osteopathy*, Colorado.

——, 1978. *Practical Osteopathic Procedures*, The Journal Printing Company, Missouri.

Mitchell, Jun., F. L., Moran, P. S. and Pruzzo, N. A., 1979. *An Evaluation and Treatment: Manual of Osteopathic Muscle Energy Procedures*, Mitchell, Moran and Pruzzo Associates, Valley Park, California.

Northup, George W., n.d. *Osteopathic Medicine: An American Reformation*, American Osteopathic Association, Chicago, Illinois.

The Northup Book: A Memorial Tribute to Thomas L. Northup, DO, 1983. American Academy of Osteopathy, Colorado.

Rowett, H. G. Q., 1959. Basic Anatomy and Physiology, John Murray, London.

Schooley, T. F., 1970. 'The Osteopathic Lesion', *Year Book of the American Academy of Osteopathy*, Colorado.

Steiner, Charles, 1977. 'The Ambulatory Treatment of the Disc Syndrome', *Year Book of the American Academy of Osteopathy*, Colorado.

Still, A. T., 1908, *Autobiography*, published privately, Kirksville, Missouri; reprinted in 1981 by the American Academy of Osteopathy, Colorado.

——, 1910. *Osteopathy, Research and Practice*, published privately, Kirksville, Missouri.

——, 1977. *Philosophy of Osteopathy*, American Academy of Osteopathy, Colorado, new edition.

Stoddard, Alan, 1959. *Manual of Osteopathic Technique*, Hutchinson and Co., London.

——, 1969. *Manual of Osteopathic Practice*, Hutchinson and Co., London.

Tortora, Gerard J. and Anagnostakos, Nicholas P., 1981. *Principles of Anatomy and Physiology*, Harper and Row, New York.

Upledger, John E. and Vredevoogd, Jon D., 1983. *Craniosacral Therapy*, Eastland Press, Chicago, Illinois.

Walter, Georgia Ann, 1981. *Osteopathic Medicine Past and Present*, College of Osteopathic Medicine, Kirksville, Missouri.

Ward, Lowell E., 1980. *The Dynamics of Spinal Stress*, SSS Press, Long Beach, California.

Wernham, John and Waldman, Mervyn, 1983. *An Illustrated Manual of Osteopathic Technique*, vol. 11, Maidstone Osteopathic Clinic, Kent.

INDEX

Page numbers in *italic* type refer to illustrations.